We rarely fully explore the healing power c  day lives, so John Steward's deeply personal, forgiveness in the midst of the Rwandan genocide is unimaginable. The personal journeys of pain and reconciliation will break your heart and inspire you. This book, emerging from experience with World Vision staff and the communities they touched, will change your perspective on the human condition.

Kevin J. Jenkins
President and Chief Executive Officer, World Vision International

John Steward's book provides a powerful and moving account of how recovery after genocide is possible. He inspires us with the stories of Rwandans who have been able to face their past and find hope in the future as they discover the potential for forgiveness and healing.

Dr Wendy Lambourne
Senior Lecturer and Deputy Director,
Centre for Peace and Conflict Studies
University of Sydney, Australia

This work makes my life richer. It is lodged in my head and heart, helping me to have hope in a world that if viewed through the headlines alone would make us all feel like Nietzsche's children.

Dr Rachael Kohn
Producer & Presenter of ABC Radio's *The Spirit of Things*, Sydney, Australia

An excellent view into an incredibly difficult passage of time, people brought so fearfully low but through a pathway of healing and forgiveness fresh life has come. Rich with insight. How easily a mostly male group can come under the domination of leaders to do the vilest deeds. People enabled to live freed of the terrible burden of unforgiveness, emerge from the darkness into a beautiful light.

Heather Jephcott
Poet and author of *Open Hearts, Quiet streams*, Indonesia

I am delighted to commend John's book *From Genocide to Generosity* for telling the personal stories of women as well as men. The direct testimonies of so many Rwandans provide powerful insights into the trauma of the genocide and speak directly of the journeys of healing and reconciliation that are so triumphant.

Professor Shirley Randell
Managing director of SRIA Rwanda Ltd
Educator in gender and the development of women in Rwanda since 2006

This history takes you on a journey of forgiveness with many open hearted Rwanda people who have faced extraordinary hardship and loss. The power of this story lies in the intimate, excruciating and heartfelt words of those who have faced horror first hand and now generously share their healing journeys. It is in their simple telling of the most difficult truths that forgiveness comes to life.

Dr Jill Parris
Counselling psychologist working specifically with trauma,
jillparris.com

While there are many different approaches to help people heal, reconcile and transform, the innovative and insightful personal narratives provided by John in this book offer a chance for many who have experienced horror the world over to not only understand, but reorganize their senses for a self that was wounded, broken and lost but can now be reclaimed. I fully endorse this book as a perfect companion for anyone seeking to reclaim their life from the devastating impacts of human-generated trauma.

Susan Wachira
Psychologist, Psychosocial Support Centre, Nairobi, Kenya
Secretary of the Kenya Counsellor and Psychological Association

If Rwandans can heal, who cannot? Perhaps their journey is showing the way to our own bright future. From that place in time to our own, let the song be sung.

Dr Alexander Shaia
Speaker and author of
Heart and Mind: the Four Gospel Journey of Transformation, USA

A truly inspiring and eye-opening book with its simple, true stories of genuine forgiveness and healing. I recommend this unique book to anyone seeking real forgiveness, healing and reconciliation – seeking to find a more ideal world in which we could live as human beings.

Nyok Gor
Peace Advocate and Co-Founder
South Sudan-Australia Peace Initiative, Melbourne

The Rwandan genocide shows the darkest hues of human madness. This book, about that crisis, shows the power of forgiveness and healing. John Steward was there and this account offers the hope that madness is not the last word – reconciliation is!

Emeritus Professor Charles Ringma
Theologian, writer and activist
Author of *Hear the Ancient Wisdom*

John Steward is a faithful and wonderful storyteller. Recounting our story is what has kept many of us Rwandans in our sanity despite the unimaginable cruelties we witnessed. In Rwanda, we talk but we are not very good at writing. This book celebrates those 'heroes' who will never write their own stories and serves the whole world by showing that there is hope even after the furnace of genocide.

Rev Antoine Rutayisire
Genocide survivor, teacher, preacher and promoter of
National Unity and Reconciliation in Rwanda

Violence is right at the heart of the human condition. The message of salvation is to move from brokenness to wholeness, to reconciliation. The miracle of forgiveness in Rwanda opens space for profound reversals. Such people who forgive the ultimate loss and create empathy instead of conflict, are incredibly challenging for us all. This is a profound book.

Rev Tim Costello
CEO, World Vision Australiai

From Genocide to Generosity

Langham
GLOBAL LIBRARY

From Genocide to Generosity

Hatreds Heal on Rwanda's Hills

John Steward

Langham

GLOBAL LIBRARY

© 2015 by John Steward

Published 2015 by Langham Global Library
an imprint of Langham Creative Projects

Langham Partnership
PO Box 296, Carlisle, Cumbria CA3 9WZ, UK
www.langham.org

ISBNs:
978-1-78368-883-8 Print
978-1-78368-056-6 Mobi
978-1-78368-055-9 ePub
978-1-78368-057-3 PDF

British Library Cataloguing in Publication Data

Steward, John, 1945- author.
  From genocide to generosity : hatreds heal on Rwanda's
  hills.
  1. Peace-building--Rwanda. 2. Genocide survivors--
  Rwanda--Attitudes.
  I. Title
  303.6'9'0967571-dc23
  ISBN-13: 9781783688838

Book Design: projectluz.com
Cover Design: Annthea Hick of ahcreative.com.au

About the cover:
The small red object on the cover art is the Rwandan Agaseke or wedding basket: a Rwandan symbol of generosity and gratitude. These pagoda-shaped baskets are sometimes called "Wedding" or "Giving" baskets. Intricately woven of delicate, naturally dyed papyrus, grass and raffia, the pattern symbolizes the journey of women walking together, sharing secrets and bearing gifts of grain, coffee or tea. The Agaseke Basket is so endemic to Rwanda that it is featured in the national seal (coat of arms) and on Rwandan currency – a symbol of hope for a brighter future. The Agaseke Basket is still a traditional and prized wedding gift, from the rural villages to the most sophisticated urbanites of Kigali. In this book it symbolizes a fresh start – being woven (bound) together; a fitting symbol of peace for Rwanda.

Photograph of John Steward © Lyndon Mechielsen

CONTENTS

I dedicate this book to the many in Rwanda
who are yet to find healing and come to peace

Foreword

We owe a huge debt of gratitude to John, and to his Rwandese companions on the way, for the enduring precious gift of *From Genocide to Generosity*.

I love the way John begins with self-disclosure about his own messed-up-ness and the contribution Rwanda has made to his own healing journey. This also serves to underline the common humanity we all share. We all have the same ability to do good and to do evil.

This book gives us a qualitative insight into the healing journey of a few individuals and the enduring impact, across time, of that transformation. It is a testimony to many remarkable and inspiring people.

As well as many new and fresh insights, *From Genocide to Generosity* confirmed me in my understandings of the process of healing, gleaned from doing Healing of Memories work across the world.

As happened each time I visited Rwanda, the book confronted me as a human being and as a person of faith . . . not least seeing that genocide happened on the altars of churches.

Many will be helped on their own journey of healing by this book. It deserves to become essential and required reading for those who would be the healers of others.

John's Dedication, and the cautionary note at the end of the book, is important: namely that healing has not happened yet for many, many Rwandese.

As John concludes, while Rwanda does not provide a recipe, "I am certain that the principles of recovery in Rwanda translate into principles of prevention and cure for the rest of us."

Fr Michael Lapsley SSM
Institute for Healing of Memories, Cape Town.

Foreword

Rwanda

0 10 20 30km

UGANDA

TANZANIA

VOLCANOES
NATIONAL
PARK

•Byumba

AKAGERA

Ruhengeri

Gisenyi

•Nyarutovu

DEMOCRATIC
REPUBLIC OF
THE CONGO

Lake Kivu

KIGALI

•Gitarama

Nyamata

THE BUGESERA

TANZANIA

•Cyangugu

NYUNGWE

Butare

BURUNDI

Prologue

*"When you want to be healed you take medicine –
and most medicines are not sweet"*

Buhanda of Ukuri Kuganze

Before Rwanda: Encountering the Violence Within

Eighteen months before moving to Rwanda, Africa, my wife, Sandi, shocked me by saying, "I am finding life with you to be most difficult and I am running out of patience. You need to work on your attitudes and how you relate to others."

Her words prompted me to take serious action, as I was proud of our twenty-seven years of marriage. A psychologist friend recommended the "Men Exploring Non-violent Solutions" workshop. For sixteen months, I attended this weekly group for men who wanted to improve their relationships. A skillful process of small group discussion invited me to be truthful and honest. I looked at aspects of my upbringing, parental models and expectations and their impact on my attitudes and behavior. I explored memories of grief and loss and discovered personal wounds, which subconsciously, had influenced me.

As a weekly homework assignment, I informed my wife about the focus and content of the latest session and invited her to describe how she experienced me in that area of my life – socially, spiritually, financially, emotionally, intimately. I listened to her response without reacting or responding, taking note of her comments and bringing these insights to our next meeting. Over the weeks, I gained new awareness into my behavior as I began to feel deeply the effects of my past actions and attitudes upon my wife, daughters and acquaintances.

Of the fifty men in the group, many had been court-ordered: they could either attend this course for two years or serve a jail sentence. Their physical aggression and violence had damaged their relationships and divided their families. I was grateful that my "wake-up call" had come before it was too late for my marriage and family.

Although my way of being was subtler than most of these men, the cause of my inappropriate behavior was similar to theirs: inner wounding that needed to be healed and would not go away on its own. I had been formed by two common beliefs: "You can't trust your feelings" and "Strong feelings can damage relationships." Yet I came to enjoy the group's focus on emotions and understanding feelings. Along with many of the other men, I became aware of self-blame and shame, suppressed emotions, ignored or devalued feelings and an unwillingness to forgive. We also discussed alternatives of healthy behavior, such as openness, respect, time-out, forgiveness and apology. I learned to speak more truthfully without manipulation.

I learned that anger was a product of an unacknowledged feeling beneath the surface. Whether the anger was passive (a feeling of tightness in the chest or stomach) or aggressive (energy in verbal or physical aggression), if I took the time to explore what was beneath my anger, I could gain insight about the attitude or experience that needed my attention.

As I began to practise identifying the feelings beneath my anger, Sandi and I visited a celebrated garden. Dozens of visitors had filled most of the parking spaces, but I spotted one in the distance. I asked Sandi to drive the car toward it while I ran and stood in the spot to reserve it. A few minutes later, my wife walked up to me and said, "I found another spot – you don't need to keep this space anymore." Instantly, anger rose up within me, and as was my habit, I went quiet. We walked in silence around the garden for an hour. I could not speak.

As we drove away, Sandi broke the silence: "I know you've been studying anger as the second feeling, and what I did earlier upset you. Have you been able to identify the deeper feeling?"

Within seconds I replied, "The first feeling is betrayal. You agreed to drive the car to the spot where I was standing, but you did not. Not only was I upset, so were the other drivers whom I stopped from taking the space. They were upset at me, and I was angry at you. You did not stick with our agreement to work together."

"That is true," she agreed, and apologized.

As we moved along in the slow traffic, I had time to look back at how I had fumed throughout the last hour. By paying attention to my feelings, I noticed how my anger subsided and then vanished. I realized that my feelings had told me that there was something that needed my attention. If I attended to a positive feeling, I could hold and enjoy it. But if I attended to a negative feeling, then I needed to acknowledge it and explore the root cause. Once I attended to the root, the negative feeling evaporated. I realized that every feeling has a role to play, either in caution or celebration.

As I began to accept responsibility for the changes I needed to make in my own life, I was amazed by how I became lighter in spirit and more able to forgive others and myself. My expectations became more realistic and I was more willing to show interest in others. But, at first, it was daunting, hard work. My faith was tested, as was my commitment to marriage. We have now been married since 1968.

Bearing Witness to Healing

During the men's group meetings, I also observed signs of healing in the other participants. Sometimes, I would come to our weekly meeting and notice a difference in the facial expressions or body language of one of the other men. "It seems like something changed for you this week," I would say. Invariably, the man would respond with surprise. "Yes, it has – but how do you know?"

"You're more relaxed," I would say – or more peaceful, gentle, or confident. As I noticed emotional transformation in others, I saw some of the same changes occur within me.

Although I did not realize it at the time this practice of observing others' emotional healing provided the foundation for much of my work in Rwanda's recovery from genocide. Through my experience with the men's group, I knew it would be important to be sensitive to what emotional changes were beginning in the people I met and to affirm those changes as I observed them. In the Prologue I will shortly explain about my going to Rwanda but before that, I give one example of the value of this sensitivity there.

While participating in my first healing workshop in Rwanda, I watched a miraculous transformation occur within the emotional mindset of a somber young woman named Drusilla. Over the nine days of the healing workshop, Drusilla had neither smiled nor frowned, and her mouth barely moved when she spoke. Her face seemed frozen. Then, during a session on forgiveness, we were given the task to personally reflect on something for which we found it hard to forgive ourselves. Drusilla said, "That's easy for me. I am responsible for the death of my younger brother. I can never forgive myself for that terrible event."

Our small group asked her to explain what she meant. She replied:

> When the genocide began, my brother wanted to run away to Burundi, but I said, 'No, the government radio is telling us to

stay at home'. This was a trick to keep people in their place while killers with lists of names and addresses went from house to house to corner their victims. So he listened to me. We stayed at home and two days later he was dead. I was responsible for the death of my brother. How can I ever forgive myself for that?

An awkward silence settled over us. We in our small group had never faced a moment like this and were uncertain what to say. Then tentatively, feeling our way, we began to ask her simple questions: Did you call the killers? Did you want them to come? Were you pleased that they came? Did you wish this to befall your brother? Did you in any way plan or desire it?

To every question, after a thoughtful pause, Drusilla responded, "No." After 15 minutes of this cautious enquiry, she looked up at us and said, "So I was not responsible for the death of my brother, was I?" It was both a question and a conclusion. As a group, we held our breath in relief and nodded in silent affirmation. As Drusilla's body felt the impact of her words, the strain on her face began to dissolve. I noticed that the muscles of her jaw began to move, the lines in her cheeks began to soften, her eyebrows arched, and she pursed her lips in relief.

During the lunch break, I observed Drusilla from a distance. As she stood under a tree, I saw her smile – perhaps her first smile in three years. Slowly her whole face became relaxed, even a little confident. I thought to myself, "I am watching a miracle taking place – this woman is healing from the inside. Self-forgiveness is setting her free from the pain and guilt that has imprisoned her."

Several weeks later, when I visited the region where Drusilla worked, she greeted me with a warm smile. We embraced in the Rwandan way, gently touching cheek to cheek and hands to hands. When later we discussed her healing, she said that for three years, her mother had pestered her about her deep sadness, saying, "You never show any signs of joy or pleasure. You never want to celebrate anything. You have become such a sad person." After completing the workshop, her mum said, "Drusilla, now you are different, you're coming alive." Drusilla's truthful answers to some simple questions from fellow-sufferers in the journey from pain to healing and forgiveness had given her the insight she needed to accept the truth that had eluded her. When she finally forgave herself, her body relaxed and relieved itself of the great burden of guilt she had been carrying.

[handwritten margin note: They allowed her to reach the conclusion]

Into Rwanda

In 1997 a Mennonite friend recommended that I apply to coordinate some NGO reconciliation and peacebuilding work in Rwanda. After assessing the position description and Rwanda's desperate need for recovery in that country, and talking with Sandi, I applied. The policy of the Rwandan Ministry of Social Affairs was to limit expatriates to a term of one or two years, in order to ensure employment for national staff. Once I was granted the position, Sandi and I began to make preparations to leave Australia. During that time a friend I had not seen for many months came to me, brimming over with excitement,

> "I hear you are about to go overseas."
> I nodded, and said "To Rwanda."
> "Where are you going to wander?" he asked.
> "Not wander – R-wanda," I replied, emphasizing the R.
> "Oh," he said, his face creasing into a perplexed frown, "Why would you want to go there?"

Days later, I received the following message from the group inviting me to Rwanda. "You need to know that in the past few weeks eight foreign expatriate aid workers have been killed in Rwanda. Be aware that the place is neither stable nor safe. We recommend you reconsider your application to join us; we offer you the option of withdrawing from your contract now, rather than coming and regretting it." My wife Sandi and I took time to reflect on the situation. We chose to continue our preparation to leave Australia and move to Rwanda.

Everyone I talked with agreed there was a lot to do if Rwanda was going to recover. The post-genocide situation was a cauldron of fear, anxiety, bitterness, pain, shame, disappointment, shock, uncertainty, poverty and confusion. As part of my pre-departure preparation, I met with three Rwandans living in Australia. The first said, "You will love Rwanda. It's very quiet now. You can go anywhere you want and you will be safe." The second one informed, "You will be dealing with people who have no trust in human beings."

The third one advised:

> Do not try to work out who is who. If you line up ten Rwandans, you can correctly guess the two at the end on the right are Tutsi and the two at the end on the left are Hutu. But of the other six you will have no idea. Intermarriage makes it impossible to guess the ethnicity of Rwandans according to their physical

appearance. Don't rely on the stereotype based on body height and nose shape.

In order to relate to every Rwandan as a human person, I decided never to ask anyone directly about their ethnicity. I would observe, listen and make up my mind, but I would not make a person's ethnicity an issue in how I saw them or related to them.

Once Sandi and I decided to go to Rwanda, we put our house in order and placed it on the rental market. When an agent found a renter, we had to move out, even though we were still waiting for our Rwandan visa and work permit. Over the next seven weeks, we became dependant on others for our housing, staying in twelve homes and storing our possessions in our car. Though this time of dislocation took place during a season of good Melbourne weather and we were fortunate to be living in a stable society, we learned to value this experience as another aspect of our preparation for Rwanda. For in a small way, we had felt up-rooted, homeless, dependant on others and not in control of our daily living, along with the Rwandans whom we were soon to meet. The intersection between the changes in my life and the amazing transformation of the Rwandans I met has prompted me to write this volume.

Introduction

"Much of Africa is on the wrong bus . . . while allowing others to lead them further from their desired destination."

Wangari Maathai

The Rwandan Genocide

In early April 1994, violence and slaughter erupted in the tiny land-locked country of Rwanda and continued for the next one hundred days, leaving up to one million Rwandans rotting in the roads and fields, buried in shallow graves, or thrown into swamps or rivers.[1] Using traditional handheld weapons and imported machetes, army, militia, neighbors and, at times, even family members attacked and killed their fellow Rwandans.

The impact of the Rwandan genocide was equivalent to the human losses and infrastructure damage of three collapses of the Twin Towers in New York, every day, for one hundred consecutive days with no rescue crews or emergency assistance for the wounded. As one missionary priest said in an interview with *TIME* magazine shortly after the genocide began, "There are no devils left in hell – they are all in Rwanda."[2]

For those Rwandans who survived these months of horror, life at times was fearful. The toll continued to rise as the Rwanda Patriotic Front (RPF), a liberation army first formed in Uganda, repelled the Rwandan Hutu government army and the *interahamwe* youth. Over these three months, almost two million Hutus and some Tutsi fled for fear of reprisals into Zaire (now Congo), Burundi and Tanzania. Thousands died in refugee camps due to the epidemics of disease and malnutrition while power struggles in the camps induced more conflict. The suffering continued for two years – and some would say it never left eastern Congo. In 1994 Saidi fled from Rwanda to Tanzania with his family. Six years later, at a refugee camp there he told a UN worker, "My wife just gave birth and is too sick to wash our child. I will tell my daughter that Rwanda was cursed by evil leaders, causing us to become

---

1. The current figure used in Rwanda is now over 1 million because many bodies were recovered from graves which perpetrators revealed when making confessions.
2. *TIME*, May 16, 1994.

refugees. Two of my children were killed there, and I will never return. I can't take another child back there to be killed. But this is not a place for a child to become a human being either."[3]

Between mid-1994 and late-1996, Rwanda was in an uneasy vacuum, half empty, half alive and moving at half speed as it struggled its way out of the morass. Beginning in 1997, with around 8 million people back in the country, Rwanda began to come to life. But it was a sobering situation – two-thirds of the adults were women and a half a million of these were widows, mostly victims of violence and rape and often infected with HIV/AIDS. Around 300,000 orphans and displaced children survived and lived without adult support in child-headed households where the oldest members of the families were teenagers. How did this all come about?

The People of Rwanda

In regard to writings on Rwanda, we hear so much about ethnicity, tribal difference and historic hatreds between traditional enemies. It is as if ideologies of difference existed long before the arrival of the colonial powers. But Rwandans say it differently; as, for example, Laurent Mbanda puts it:

> Rwanda is home to a people called the Banyarwanda, who embrace three groups – Hutu, Tutsi and Twa – of the same nation. . . . Although these groups have been referred to as ethnic or tribal groups . . . Rwandan elders believe that these three groups are one people with a common ancestry. . . .The emphasis was on what they shared instead of what might divide them. The unique proof of that is the Banyarwanda living in the same village houses next to one another for centuries, sharing a common language and culture.[4]

Church adds that Rwandans shared all the wealth of their traditional way of life " . . . with its folklore, ballads, music and dances, its arts and crafts."[5] Mbanda suggests that in pre-colonial Rwanda the most visible difference was occupation. The royal family, nobles, commanders, many chiefs and people who kept cattle were (Aba)Tutsi; the (Aba)Hutu were farmers and the (Aba)Twa were a minority group of hunters and pottery makers. Hutu

---

3. *COLORS* 41:Refugees 2000, Italy.

4. Laurent Mbanda, *Committed to Conflict* (London: SPCK, 1997), 3.

5. J. E. Church, *Forgive Them: The Story of an African Martyr* (London: Hodder & Stoughton, 1966), 58.

could become Tutsi and vice-versa, so the terms refer not to origin but social condition. Intermarriage was a long-standing practise.

The German colonialists, supported by western anthropologists, first promoted the superiority of the Tutsi over the Hutu, while also proposing that the former came to Rwanda from Ethiopia. After the Germans lost their colony to Belgium in 1914, the latter maintained a preference for educating and employing Tutsi of certain clans. The Belgian government, with the support of Catholic missionary and church leaders, promoted these Tutsi as superior and more worthy of education and civil employment, so planting seeds of bias and preference. In 1933 the Belgians introduced ethnicity on an identity card, which adult Rwandans were obliged to carry. This colonial mechanism became a basis for one grouping to exercise power over the other.

Alison Des Forges of Human Rights Watch writes:

> This distorted version of the past told more about the intellectual atmosphere of Europe in the 1920s than about the early history of Rwanda…In Rwanda it was disseminated through the schools and seminaries…(and) stood unchallenged until the 1960s, when a new generation of scholars…began questioning some of its basic assumptions.[6]

Nevertheless interdependence remained alive and enabled Hutu to trade their labour and crops with the Tutsi in exchange for milk and cattle.

The Slide towards Genocide

Significant uprisings and attacks on civilians began in 1959, resulting in the exile of many. According to Tom Ndahiro from that time " . . . successive governments maintained that the Tutsi were foreigners who needed to be eradicated. Killing Tutsi by throwing them into the Nyabarongo River was considered part of sending them back to their purported origin – Ethiopia, via the River Nile."[7]

In 1962, Rwanda became a Republic and held democratic elections, giving the power to prioritize Hutus in education and government. Church leaders also changed allegiance from Tutsi to Hutu, and Tutsi gradually fell to the margins of society. Yet, for years to come, many Rwandans co-existed

---

6. Alison Des Forges, *Leave none to tell the story* (New York: Human Rights Watch, 1999), 37.
7. Tom Ndahiro, "Genocide Laundering," in *After Genocide: Transitional Justice, Post-conflict Reconstruction and Reconciliation in Rwanda and Beyond*, eds. Philip Clark and Zachary D. Kaufman (London: Hurst, 2008), 114.

harmoniously with neighbours.[8] Cycles of violence in Rwanda catalysed the formation of an army of the RPF, consisting of Rwandans in exile who supported Yoweri Museveni's rise to power in Uganda.

In late 1990 this army began incursions into Rwanda along the southern border of Uganda, signalling their desire to return home. This was rebuffed on the grounds that Rwanda's population already filled available land. In August 1993, as a result of the persistence of the RPF, and support from within Rwanda, a power-sharing agreement was signed in Arusha between the Rwandan Hutu President Habyarimana and RPF representatives. But the President delayed implementing the agreement, being overtaken by "members of the fanatical, despotic Akazu clan directed by (Habyarimana's wife) Agathe and her brothers."[9] They worked with intellectuals to develop an ideology to formalise genocide and made plans to implement a 'final solution'. The Genocide of the Tutsi began on April 7, 1994 after the downing of the plane that killed the Presidents of Rwanda and Burundi.

At that time, one million Tutsi and moderate Hutu were living in long-term exile in Europe and in Africa: Uganda, Burundi, Kenya and Tanzania. Many of them longed to return home. The opportunity came three months later when the RPF captured Kigali on July 19th, 1994 and the genocidal government fled. A new Government of Rwanda was sworn in and the rebuilding began.

Neither tribalism nor ethnic differences were the reason for the genocide in Rwanda. The violent explosion was preceded by numerous mounting tensions: population density and pressure for land, low literacy, an unwillingness to forgive, unresolved hurt, threats and accusations, church leaders' desire for political influence and lack of resolve to speak out, the promotion of group interest above community unity, cycles of revenge and killing with impunity, fears, party propaganda etc. However, ultimately, it happened because "the genocide was well planned."[10]

Indifference of the West

While genocide raged, the UN failed to send additional peacekeepers. The United States dragged its feet because it did not want a repeat of the

---

8. See for example chapter 2 of Frida Gashumba, *Frida: Chosen to Die, Destined to Live* (Lancaster: Sovereign World, 2007), 26–36.

9. Ryszard Kapuściński, *The Shadow of the Sun* (London: Penguin Books, 2001),178.

10. Fergal Keane, *Season of Blood: A Rwandan Journey* (London: Viking, 1995), 9.

embarrassing debacle of its forces in Somalia in 1993.[11] The small UN peacekeeping force stationed in Kigali was hampered by its limited powers. Lieutenant General Roméo Dallaire argued that 5,000 extra troops could have restricted the number of deaths.[12] But his appeal for reinforcements fell on deaf ears. In contrast to the impressive and powerful response to the war in Kosovo, the so-called 'civilized world' looked the other way and let the Rwandan genocide happen.[13]

Later, in his preface to an Anthology discussing issues related to post-genocide Rwanda and transitional justice, Rwandan President Paul Kagame wrote:

> The 1994 genocide in Rwanda is a blight on all of humanity. The world's failure to intervene to halt the genocide has scarred the world's conscience and begs serious questions about the role of the UN and other international actors in resolving conflict. We must not forget what Rwandans experienced in 1994, what the perpetrators did, and what the international community failed to do.[14]

An Uncertain Peace

In late 1994 many of the Rwandans who had taken refuge in neighbouring African countries began to return, bringing the education and business skills they gained during exile. They also carried years of pain and sadness after living as unwanted 'foreigners', in addition to the memories of persecution, pressure and danger, which had led their parents to flee Rwanda from the 1950s onward. These returnees added to the complexity of a battered country and its shattered people.

Many of the long-term exiles moved onto properties that had been recently abandoned by those fleeing the country to escape the consequences of genocide. But, from late 1996 to early 1997 the two million Hutu (and Tutsi) short-term refugees left their camps in Congo and walked back en-masse to Rwanda. Upon reaching their homes and gardens they found a

---

11. The positive impact upon Rwandans by the apology of President Clinton at the Kanombe airport in 1998 surprised me.

12. Roméo Dallaire, *Shake Hands with the Devil* (Toronto: Random House, 2003), 356 & 359.

13. I recommend that travellers to Rwanda make it a priority to visit the Genocide Memorial Centre at Gisozi. This helps visitors to understand both the richness of the Rwandan past, the complexity of the whole story and the pathos and tragedy of the human losses. Learn more at www.genocidearchiverwanda.org.rw

14. Paul Kagame, "Preface," in *After Genocide*, eds. Philip Clark and Zachary D. Kaufman (London: Hurst, 2008), xxvi.

generation of un-familiar and un-welcome exiles. This new challenge added to the uneasy calm in Rwanda, and while the new government developed its vision and found its feet, it soon began building programs to accommodate those who were homeless.

Encountering Rwanda

This was the crucible I faced when we touched down at Kigali airport one quiet Sunday morning in March 1997. As we taxied from the airport into Kigali, I looked out the window, surveying our new 'home', taking note of the bullet holes in the airport terminal and the national Parliament, grenade marks on the roads and the twisted hulks of a few rusted cars. As Sandi and I settled into our accommodation, I listened to the clap-clap-clap of shuffling sandals as people moved along the roadside to church. From our window, I could see people crammed together in the valleys of Kigali, shrouded in cloud and wisps of smoke, huddled beneath simple structures with rusting roofs and mud-splattered walls. All along the red-brown earthen paths, I watched women carrying vessels of water on their heads, shoulders and arms. Youth pedalled past them, balancing water jugs on their bicycles.

As I walked through the streets, many of the people passed by as if we were not there – an unusual phenomenon for Africa which gave me an eerie feeling in the headache-inducing, high altitude air. Black Kites glided in mesmerising sweeps high above mounds of rubbish in the streets. Crows and street urchins sifted through the fresher piles of waste material. A few kids called out, 'muzungu' (white or wealthy man) or 'bis-kwit' when they saw me, as for many weeks the long walk of refugees returning from Congo had been assisted by roadside gifts of protein-enriched biscuits from foreign NGO staff. In the late afternoon, guards in dark garments with rifles at their side paced backward and forward in the dim light, with few other humans moving along the street. By nightfall, apart from military patrols, the streets of Kigali were deserted.

As I looked at the heavy, sombre faces of the Rwandan people, I felt relatively untouched by the trauma and tragedy that had struck them. I was also quite uncertain about what the experience would hold. A few days later I heard a friend refer to the many traumatized Rwandans as 'The Walking Dead.' At that moment, I realized that I was not encountering a theoretical situation, but a scale of devastation that I had never imagined before leaving Australia.

A few weeks after landing in Rwanda, I came across a 1996 report from the Harvard Program of Refugee Trauma, highlighting two factors for everyone living in Rwanda – Tutsi, Hutu and Twa alike.[15] First, the report identified that Rwanda was facing a mental health crisis.

> Rwandan citizens have experienced the following major types of traumatic events: family member killed, family member died from disease, friend killed, relative or friend disappeared, separation from family, forced evacuation, destruction of home, farm or neighbourhood, destruction of church, school, injuries, leaving all, returning to the country, feeling that one's life is in danger, physically assaulted, hiding for long periods, long periods without food, betrayal by neighbours or friends.

Second, the report noted that many Rwandans had experienced not one, but *all*, of these traumatic events.

> No Rwandan, whether Hutu or Tutsi, has been left untouched by the recent violence. The cumulative effect of mass violence in Rwanda will be to have generated hundreds of thousands of individuals who are suffering from the medical and emotional sequelae of torture, physical injury, and psychological harm . . . those citizens who are 'damaged' but 'functioning' must all find a sensitivity to their efforts and minimum resources to help them sustain their resiliency.

Setting the report aside, I began to wonder if perhaps I had come in too much haste. I felt emotionally raw and mentally unprepared for the complicated and arduous task set before me to encourage healing and the building of peaceful relationships.

Yet because my own life had been transformed for the good and I had seen transformation among some of the men in my healing workshop, I felt confident that recovery might be possible for Rwandans, even though they had experienced horrific trauma. I had also seen hope emerge in other countries devastated by violence, and so I felt determined to honour my call to Rwanda and give the hope for healing and restoration a try. There would be no going back, but I knew I would need inspiration and guidance each step along the way.

Looking Ahead

From Genocide to Generosity focuses on the journey of healing revealed in a handful of brave people whose generosity has become a catalyst for change

---

15. *The Crisis in Rwanda*, Harvard Program of Refugee Trauma, 1996.

in the lives of hundreds of fellow Rwandans since the genocide of 1994. In the following six parts, I trace my journey in coming to understand more deeply the complex situation of Rwanda, and I also outline the resources that guided the work of restoration. More importantly, I introduce you to several Rwandans who, through their own experiences of healing, eventually became facilitators in the healing of others.

Part 1: *Coping with Chaos*, describes what I came to understand about Rwanda by listening to and learning from the Rwandan people. I also describe the work of Professor Simon Gasibirege, a Rwandan whose personal healing in Europe helped him develop a series of healing workshops that has impacted thousands and continues to offer new hope to many today.

Part 2: *Looking for Light*, introduces two of my Rwandan colleagues who were survivors of the violence. Karigirwa worked resolutely at the local level among adults and children. Munyeli stepped into a role with a more regional focus. Both enabled hundreds to find a new purpose for living.

Part 3: *Taming the Trauma*, introduces Nyamutera, a young Hutu who did not participate in the genocide, but who fled into the refugee camps of Congo. He returned to Rwanda, bitter, confused and disillusioned. His healing came through a workshop developed by a Welsh doctor, Rhiannon Lloyd. Nyamutera began to co-lead this workshop for clergy, priests and lay-leaders, impacting hundreds of Rwandans in leadership.

Part 4: *Hope after the Horror*, introduces my Rwandan colleagues Nsabiyera and Jean-Baptiste, who followed the stories of grassroots change from the two workshops introduced in Parts Two and Three. Nsabiyera's thoughtful analysis deepens our understanding of healing within Rwanda, while Jean -Baptiste weaves in the interfaith contribution of Fr Michael Lapsley from South Africa. This process expanded the healing work in Rwanda.

In Part 5: *Judging for Justice*, we follow Munyeli's work to educate communities in preparation for the justice trials, which were adapted from the traditional conflict resolution process called the *gacaca* (grassroots). Through these local tribunals, over 400,000 cases of involvement in the genocide were brought to justice. In a world first, the whole country was involved in grassroots restorative justice, without the involvement of lawyers.

Part 6: *Facing the Future*, introduces Ikiriza and her work with more than two thousand youth who expressed their hopes for a peaceful Rwanda through indigenous art forms, such as music, dance, drama and poetry. I describe the peaceful future envisioned by the youth as they performed their songs, dances and dramas with diverse audiences.

I conclude, in the *Epilogue*, with the signs of life in the new Rwanda and outline some of the challenges which remain in the country. I also reflect on the plea of my Rwandan friends: "We are recovering, we have a long way to go, but we want the world to know our hope-filled story."

Acknowledging Sources

As a promoter of healing and change, the most difficult part of this book to write was the earlier pages of this Introduction. I have few reference resources on the precolonial history and relationships in Rwanda, and the historical background is both complex and even distorted, and therefore contested among Rwandans, depending on the individual person's upbringing and education. Further exploration beckons all readers who find unsatisfying the relatively sparse lines I offer.

Turning to my main focus, I learned to love stories from my mother, who published three small books about my boyhood years, growing up in a Javanese village in the mid-1950s. The value of stories as a source of wisdom and insight became clear to me while I was working in rural community development in Asia during the 1970s through 1990s. Three storytellers in the Philippines – James Yen, Juan Flavier and Roland Bunch – influenced my views, while Nora Avarientos, Dilsy Arbutantè and Mick Duncan took me to learn from communities who were rewriting their stories.

While working in Rwanda, stories first gave me hope that change could occur. After gathering a small team of Rwandans, we agreed to seek at least one story each per month and use it to guide our work as healers and peace builders. We would talk about those stories as part of our reflective learning and team building, and we documented them to share in reports, speaking engagements and formation programs. The insights we received from these cases prepared and motivated us to press on amidst challenging circumstances.

In doing this work we deliberately sought permission for sharing story content and direct quotes with a wider public audience. Most of our conversations were with people with whom we had nurtured relationships over a long time. At the beginning of each interview or discussion, we asked those who were sharing their stories to refrain from telling anything they wanted to keep private. My colleagues usually recorded the stories in Kinyarwanda. After writing down a verbatim record of the interview, they would translate it into English. When I was part of the interaction with a Kinyarwanda speaker, an interpreter was present. As the person was talking to the interpreter, I made detailed notes about what had already been translated, seeking to faithfully record all pertinent comments. In the filmed interviews, a Rwandan translated the script, usually within hours of filming. At the end of all our healing workshops participants filled in an evaluation, which included a section requesting a comment or impression about the workshop impact which we would be free to quote, while the source remained anonymous.

Because of my commitment to listening I preferred to let a story unfold, allowing the speaker to keep the narrative flowing without interruption. Many of the Rwandans I spoke with became friends. Thus, apart from the occasional clarifying question, I did not intrude for detail. This allowed people to speak from the heart. What we captured were vivid glimpses of the parts of their stories they wanted to share.

In preparing to write this book, I relied on notes from translated conversations and video recordings, as described above, as well as monthly written reports, formal briefings and informal verbal reports from team meetings and my journal. I also drew from articles and speeches written or delivered by teammates or close acquaintances and by myself, which focused on our personal involvement and observations. Finally, I drew from the many healing and peace-building trainings in which I participated. I have delivered over two hundred addresses about Rwanda and its healing journey and led over three hundred hours of training in ten other countries.

The source material for this book was gathered over a span of seventeen years, with the most active documentation of stories between 1997 and 2007, and later in 2012. Yet from the beginning of my journey in Rwanda in 1997 up to the present, I have continued to receive updates, additional background details and developments in stories from the many friends with whom I remain in touch. This makes it difficult to indicate a specific date for most of the particular stories. In the few cases where information was not directly obtained from the person, I indicate the source in the footnotes.

The Rwandans we meet in these pages want their stories to be known. I acknowledge my great debt to them as gracious and generous hosts and friends. Their stories illuminate a pathway towards healing and generosity. Now as we turn to Part 1, I glance back at those eerie first moments as Sandi and I walked the quiet streets of Kigali and pondered what it was like when these dusty lanes ran with tears and blood as the gathering storm which became the Rwandan genocide exploded the peace and dimmed the beauty of this colourful and alluring country.

1

Coping with Chaos

"You cannot heal what you cannot feel."

Dale Bronner

Outsider in Kigali

When I reported on my first day in Rwanda, the NGO director took me by surprise by greeting me with some crisp advice: "You have come to a very complex situation. This country is not easy to understand. Therefore please do not attempt anything for at least three months. Take time to appreciate what has been tried, what works, what has been achieved, and what needs to be done. I recommend that you do nothing but listen."

In my previous overseas assignments in aid and development work I had never been told to do nothing! The focus had always been, "Get into action and respond swiftly to human need, there's a lot to do now – urgently." This new welcome and warning was wise and timely, as it placed me in the position of a learner, rather than a leader; a friend, rather than a problem-solver. It accorded with the greeting of a Rwandan colleague, who held my left wrist, tapped my Seiko and teased, "Ah you *muzungus* – you have the watches, but we Africans have the time!"

As I met Rwandans, I was struck by their directness and the way they looked me in the eye. Person after person greeted me warmly and expressed a common sentiment, "Welcome to Rwanda. You have a most difficult job – and please don't ask me to forgive anybody." After a few days I realized they were giving me a message: "Peace and reconciliation are important, but I am not yet ready for it."

Over the next three months of visiting, listening and learning, when I asked groups about their experience of peace and reconciliation programs, all the responses had a similar tone: "We had wonderful sessions learning Rwanda's history and the causes of genocide with very interesting and experienced speakers who inspired us and helped us understand our past. Now that you've come we would like to have more of these sessions. They are important for our future." When I enquired about participants who had been impacted and if there were healing or forgiveness, they invariably replied, "You are new here, aren't you? This is Rwanda. Things like that don't happen here."

After receiving this disappointing feedback and reading the Harvard research paper about people in Rwanda swamped by trauma and living with inner turmoil, I knew we needed evidence of positive impact upon participants in peace and reconciliation programs. So I decided to wait to develop a program until I could find an approach that made a difference.

Also daunting were the daily visits to my office of men I had never before met, coming to tell me their gruesome, graphic, desperate, sad and hopeless stories. When I asked the men why they had come to talk to me, they always answered, "I do not trust any African." A short distance down the road from my office, many women came to the unit where we lived to tell their stories to Sandi. Each evening, during our walk around the neighbourhood, Sandi and I would debrief with one another, divesting ourselves of the horror, hurt and hopelessness which poured from these troubled storytellers. At this early stage, all we could do was listen, hold the stories we had heard, pray, and then let them go before sleep.

Then one day, I heard of a man who had been imprisoned for his part in the events of 1994, who had told a chaplain, "I killed a man and I am sorry that I did. Here is a note, please take it to his widow who is now in Burundi." When the woman read the letter, she said, "Oh, he's confessing and asking for forgiveness for killing my husband. That is progress. I'm going to shift back to Kigali and live near his prison. I will cook him food and take it to the jail for him – prisoners can't survive without the help of others."

Around the same time, Sandi heard about a group of widows who, despite chronic shortages, had decided to contribute half of their food to patients in the central hospital of Kigali, because what the patients were given was insufficient for their survival. Undeterred by their personal pain and the hardship of being genocide survivors, these widows walked a long distance twice each week, giving from the little they had, regardless of the ethnicity of the recipients, bathing patients who did not have any family to care for them. These stories provided hope as I persevered in my search for effective ways to rebuild peace.

Process, Journey, Possibility

My small office in Kigali was, like most in Rwanda at that time, devoid of decoration, very humble and short of resources. I was drawn to one of the few books on the shelf, written by the Mennonite psychologist David Augsburger,[1] who described "the four normal human responses to a painful experience between two parties" as denial, revenge, forgiveness and reconciliation. In developing a strategy for my work in Rwanda, I knew psycho-social healing processes would need to provide a diverse range of possibilities, with sufficient room for people to react in different ways, as Augsburger's list indicated.

I did not want people to feel pressured to respond in a particular or predetermined way. Rather, I hoped to discover African ways that would encourage honest and appropriate assessment of the situation. Some Rwandans might need to express their rage and state their desire for revenge; others might need to express their un-readiness to forgive; some might need to talk about their fear of going against the flow of their clan's opinion; others might need to talk about how to resolve the conflict with particular family enemies; some might need time to find the courage to speak the truth; others might need to find a safe place where they could confess.

In searching for such an open-ended approach, I focused on three key words: process, journey and possibility. To keep my hopes and expectations realistic, I looked for models that focused on the *process* of healing, the *journey* of forgiveness and the *possibility* of achieving reconciliation. In my search for participants, I looked for those Rwandans who were willing to be involved in the work of healing and forgiveness, as "work with the willing" was a mantra I had learned in previous community development experiences.

A Process of Healing: Denial and Revenge

Ndogoni, a Kenyan psychologist and colleague, explained to me: "Denial is healthy up to a point, because it stabilizes people who would otherwise

---

1. See David W. Augsburger, *Helping People Forgive* (Louisville: Westminster John Knox Press, 1996).

flounder in difficult circumstances." So denial is useful for surviving, but continuing in denial can create a false sense of peace. For when denial causes us to ignore pain, we tend to nurture bitterness, suppress anger and may even ferment a desire for revenge. At some point in time, if it is not dealt with through a process of healing, this inner 'fire' will express itself inappropriately – either it will consume us, or it will erupt in an act of violence or aggression against another.

For many Rwandans, denial had become a default stance. In some cases, people knew they needed help, but had nowhere to turn. Others did not want to begin healing work because their lives were focused on survival, and they had neither the time nor energy for anything else. Their guideline became: "We just have to get on with living." For some, denial was a choice. I heard one government official declare, "Sure there is a lot of pain in my life, the losses were terrible, but we can't weep about that – we have a country to rebuild. That has to be our focus." Others believed they had no need to deal with their inner issues. These prevailing attitudes prevented progress in the society as a whole.

In revenge, also called vengeance or scape-goating, the victim or survivor wants a perpetrator to suffer at least as much as they have. This is "the ancient formula for undying futility",[2] when we use our power to impose a penalty on the person or group who has hurt us – or on someone we associate with that person or group – so cementing the distance between victim and perpetrator. With this response, painful memories do not fade or disappear, but rather enlarge our thirst for revenge until we harm others with violence, poisoning, shunning, ridicule, prejudice or favouritism. All these dimensions of revenge were present in Rwanda.

A Journey towards Forgiveness

We generally find it hard to forgive ourselves when we fail to act or feel we did not do enough to prevent harm. In Rwanda, many people were haunted by hindsight feelings, such as, "I failed to protect my family," "I did not warn my friend," "We did not flee quickly enough," or "Why did I do that?" But those who acknowledged their shortcomings and chose to forgive themselves experienced inner relief from their guilt. They began to see how they had

---

2. Lewis B. Smedes, *The Art of Forgiving: When You Need to Forgive and Don't Know How* (Melbourne: Summit Publishing, 1996) 71.

blamed others for their predicament, and they acknowledged how they had shamed or wished evil on those they considered guilty.

Once we forgive ourselves, we open ourselves to the possibility of forgiving others. The act of forgiving someone else eases the tension we have been holding within ourselves due to our wish to hold others accountable for their actions. Many are surprised when they realize that the initiative to forgive benefits the forgiver and may not change the situation of the perpetrator.

The Possibility of Reconciliation

Reconciliation is a two-way interaction, wherein one party shows their repentance through an apology and an offer of justice or restitution, while the other party initiates or responds with spoken forgiveness. Forgiveness and restorative justice diffuse the negative energy between parties, enabling them to interact courteously. Reconciliation sometimes leads to a long-term relationship between the survivor and perpetrator. Because of the face-to-face interaction necessary for reconciliation, this response to hurt is relatively rare.

The Path to Healing: Begin by Walking in Another's Shoes

When I arrived in Kigali in 1997, my colleagues on the "trauma, peace and reconciliation team"[3] within our NGO had just discovered the work of Professor Simon Gasibirege, a Rwandan psychologist who had lived in exile in Belgium for over thirty years. Impressed by the healing work of Holocaust survivors, he observed how entrenched grief and pain could be processed in ways that helped victims and their descendants move out of the spiralling grip of negative emotions about what had been done to them and their relatives. A deep thinker, practical psychologist and a man of faith, Simon connected his mental health studies to his own difficult life experiences, which had exiled him from Rwanda many years earlier. In 1994, shortly after the genocide, Simon returned to Rwanda, when his people were raw and hurting. He told me:

> When I returned to Rwanda I tried to travel around in the few vehicles that were operating. It was like during winter in Europe – people's faces were closed, there were no smiles. People never talked, they were very quiet and most of them thought they'd

---

3. Hereafter referred to as the trauma team.

come to the end of their lives; they had no hope for the future. Even when they tried to talk to me they just told me what happened during the genocide.

When I walked around I saw damaged roads and buildings, and smelled stinking places because of the dead bodies. What shocked me was that most of the places seemed like a grave yard – buildings were smashed, equipment lay broken and gathering dust, gardens were destroyed. I could not hear people laughing. Poverty was all around Rwanda. I had to walk long distances; everyone was very thin.

As Simon tried to imagine others' sorrows, he began to ask himself, "What could I do to contribute towards the healing of my country?" Engaged as a Professor of Community Health at the Rwandan National University in Butare, Simon developed a Personal Development Workshop, known as the PDW, which incorporated many of the ideas that had benefitted him in Belgium.

In our interview, Simon described the workshop: "The PDW is formed in such a way that it assists people through a journey of mourning. It helps a person pass through four stages of mourning. Each stage is a separate, specific workshop."

Following is Simon's description of the first workshop stage:

During mourning a person lives without plans, so this step is about planning a way forward. We used to start with the film "Rwanda, the country that went mad." It reminded people of their need for mourning and aimed to prevent denial of how the genocide came about. We used to show the film to remember how the genocide was an event that was planned; it happened for a variety of reasons. We needed to see it was not a curse from heaven; its causes were right here on the ground.

We no longer show that film. We stopped using it in 2000. Since then, rather than one that reminds them of the genocide, we've been showing a film about Rwandans living together.

This first event is one day and serves to allow attendees to assess whether they are ready to participate and interact in small groups. Some choose not to continue. We want people to face their troubles, but it is hard for people to be confronted by their emotions. During the first stage we ask people to remember what they passed through, and what they felt at that time. This is a preparation to begin the next stage.

Following the first stage, participants took several weeks to consider if they were ready to move to the second stage. Typically, among the fifty or sixty participants, between fifteen to twenty decided they were ready to proceed. Others chose to wait until a better time. Simon describes the second stage of the workshop as follows:

> This requires each person to recall and experience the feelings they had during the war/genocide and to talk about it among other participants. The focus for these three days is bereavement, reflecting on the loved ones who departed from them and grieving their losses. Many people have not yet grieved, particularly where the bodies of their loved ones are yet to be found. They pour out their pain and anguish, often with weeping.

After the second workshop, participants returned to their normal life for one month. This allowed them to personalize their insights and gain new balance. While they continued their daily work, they took the opportunity to explain what they had learned to family, neighbours and friends. This helped to 'earth' the integration process. After this month-long break, participants gathered for the third workshop, which Simon describes below:

> This stage is about analysing the feelings, understanding them and deciding how to manage them. We have a well-known Rwandan saying: "The tears of a man flow down the inside to his stomach." This is one indication that Rwandans can be reticent to acknowledge and benefit from their inner emotions. They learn a lot about themselves and their parents in these three days. They are shown models of relating and communicating which they can practice and use to show respect towards others, whether it be a partner, child, friend, enemy or stranger.

Following the third workshop, participants took another month-long break in order to put into practice the insights they had gained during the teaching and discussions. This space gave them time to consider their new understandings, attitudes and behaviours, and experience how they were making a difference in their daily lives. Then participants gathered for the fourth and final workshop, which Simon describes below:

This stage is about learning to live with the feelings and being able to reconcile with one's self before reconciling with others. These can be a life-changing three days. Participants are surprised at the thought of needing to forgive themselves first. In this session we use a wonderful sheet to look at twelve steps of forgiveness, and participants who reach this point find the material freeing. Nobody is placed under pressure to forgive anybody. All forgiveness has to be at the right time; this is a very personal thing.[4]

As I listened to Simon, I recognized how the workshop material held a key to unravelling the knotted and repressed emotions of Rwandans. When Simon needed volunteers to test the workshop, he selected those who were ready to be open and trust others in small group work. In this way, the PDW became a form of professional development for our trauma team – with the hope that they might extend the healing they experienced to the people with whom they were working. With these healing workshops, we began our journey as a team in accompanying Rwandans towards forgiveness. Our experiences kept us hopeful about the possibility of reconciliation between some Tutsi and Hutu, perpetrator and survivor/victim.

In the meantime, as I mingled with colleagues at work, I discovered that personal issues were creating tensions in relationships. Many of the staff were from families who had originally fled Rwanda years before and carried 'scars' of trauma from living in long-term exile. There was a tendency for them to be identified with the victors, and not all people in Rwanda welcomed them back. Thus, like so many post-genocide Rwandans, their behaviour often conveyed anxious suspicion and fear around any change, as well as defensiveness, blame and counter-accusation when questioned. These dynamics made it difficult for us all, and I began to use small group work to create an environment of trust as a preparation for other colleagues to consider participating in the PDW.

Once Professor Simon's trial program received positive feedback, others began to ask for an opportunity to attend. My hopes lifted when I received a phone call from a colleague in our Nyamata office asking, "What are you doing to our staff? Since attending the workshop, one of them is smiling for the first time. Another is willing to negotiate for the first time. And a

---

4. The Appendix contains the material to which Simon referred.

third, who would only work on his own, is now cooperating with the team. Something good is happening to these staff. When is the next workshop?"

We also received moving evaluation comments from the first PDW participants, such as the excerpts below:

> I was an orphan to be pitied; I was a widow in need of grace; I was a child in need of education; I was a parent without a child to bring up. When I got the chance to participate, in the Personal Development workshop, I was relieved. I was no longer sorrowful but happy.

* * *

> I would like to write to thank you for the effort you have made to help us build up ourselves and forgive each other [through] the wonderful workshop called the PDW.
>
> These workshops helped us to know ourselves, and how we can do our bereavement, how to express our emotions and understand our feelings, and how to forgive. We have now concluded these workshops . . . and have taken decisions and made resolutions that will help us to cope with the difficulties of the life which we now live in Rwanda.

* * *

> I have decided the following things: to forgive myself, to learn to know and understand myself and to understand others, to forgive all the people with whom I have conflicts, and to reconcile myself with God so that I may be able to improve my relationship with my relatives, my neighbours, my supervisors at work and be strengthened to rebuild the country.

* * *

> Thank you for the light you gave me and I ask you to do the best you can to help us again so that we may be able to enlighten many Rwandans who have got thousands of problems and who desire to get answers to at least 999 questions in order to be able to forgive each other and live at peace in this country.

* * *

After losing all my family at the same time – every relative, all my brothers and sisters, I was confused. I felt life could not continue. I was keeping everything, all my feelings inside me. I felt so heavy. Suddenly, after the PDW, I knew where I was and where I wanted to go. I became free to respond emotionally to people, and to help neighbours. I became settled.

* * *

Oh! Let me tell you why I am very at ease within myself: I have just known what I did not know. I have understood what I did not understand. I have felt what I have never felt in me. I feel good, I am well, for this reason my burden has fallen down. Viva, these workshops.

In spite of the positive feedback, some senior staff within our NGO resisted the PDW, because they felt it took too much time and energy from their staff. I proposed to participate in the PDW in order to bring an informed 'outsider' opinion.

Coming Home in Rwanda

Sandi and I participated in a French version of the PDW, which was translated for us by Nsabiyera, a colleague from the trauma team, who processed his own past while interpreting. The other eleven participants were Hutu and Tutsi, male and female, all carrying wounding from events surrounding the genocide. Each morning, we recited 'The rules of protection', in which we committed to participate, to respect each other, to be truthful, and not be under the influence of drugs. At the end of the first daily recitation, one participant banged her fist on the table and said, "I have one more rule: I will participate in this workshop so long as I am not asked to forgive anybody. The moment I am told I must forgive somebody, I am leaving this workshop!" She stayed right through all stages, repeating her extra rule at the beginning of every day.

The bereavement session, which focused on grief and loss, encouraged us to express long-held grief. In Rwanda, despite the many deaths, survivors had put their feelings and inner lives on hold in order to take care of their survival needs. Three years after the genocide, many Rwandans continued to lock away their grief over the loss of kin, friends and colleagues, as well as property.

During one small group discussion, I listened in amazement as one Tutsi said to a Hutu, "After hearing your story and bearing in mind my own bitter experience, I realize that as a Hutu, you and your family suffered more in the long-term than I have as a Tutsi in genocide." A re-humanizing of relationships was beginning among us as a fruit of open, honest conversation.

During these sessions, I mourned the loss of my baby brother, who had died of congenital heart failure at six months. I grieved because I had never held and cuddled him, choosing to delay any close contact until he got better. For forty years, I held the pain of this grief, having lost the brother I longed for, as I grew up with five sisters. Rwandans in my group responded to this pain with surprise, "We didn't realize Westerners also suffer grief because they lost a loved one. We are touched by you sharing your suffering with us." Their empathy moved me and brought me consolation and deep inner peace, because they had suffered infinitely more than I had.

Towards the end of the workshop on grief, we composed personal letters of farewell to someone whose loss we had been holding. We wrote what we would have said to that person if we'd had a chance to say goodbye to them on the day before they died. I was able to express my long-suppressed love for my brother, which liberated my emotions and lightened my heart.

Though I came to Rwanda as an outsider, I experienced healing alongside my Rwandan brothers and sisters. In this way, I came 'home' within myself and became more human, more who I was meant to be. This unexpected outcome was an extension of the change that had begun with my men's healing group in Melbourne.

Coming home to one-self

Looking Back

Fifteen years after our first meeting in Rwanda, I asked Professor Simon to assess the impact of the PDW in Rwanda. While he could not guess how many people had participated in the PDW, he was confident that 90 percent of participants had experienced healing in some way. He noted three outcomes, depending on the individual:

> The first outcome of the PDW was that people learned to trust again – to trust themselves and to trust other people. What led to that trust was when people talked to others and learned that some were worse off than them, while others were better off.
>
> Second, people who had been unable to take decisions about getting married, even widows, were able to remarry; others

who had become alcoholics in trying to avoid and hide from their wounds, decided to stop their drinking. The healing that occurred through the workshops helped husbands reconcile with their wives and parents apologize to their children for cruel or harsh behaviour. Children who dropped out of school were able, after the PDW, to go back and study. Many children in survivor associations have spoken of their new hopes and have come to thank me.

Third, after people participated in the PDW they could express their emotions. Some people discovered that they had difficulty making decisions, because they kept their emotions inside their heart. When we know and use our emotions well, they bring good energy. When we can express them and speak about them with other people, emotions are good energy. When we cannot express them or speak about them with other people, they become negative energy, which cannot be expressed through speech, or in relationship with others. Then these negative energies in the body search for a way in which they can come out. They are expressed in destructive ways and in the process they destroy the body.

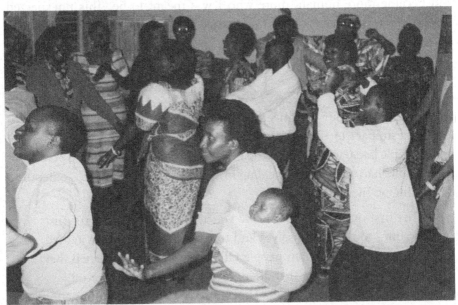

Group celebrating completion of a PDW   © John Steward

When they can speak about their emotions with other people, and other people can speak to them, they change. Relationship centres on the emotions in each person, so emotions are expressed in speech between people in relationship. This is the healthy way of relating. But before participating in the workshop, they could not do it, so the emotions remained in the body, and they can destroy the body – through psychosomatic disease.

Eye-Witness to Transformation

During my PDW, I observed deep change and the beautiful birthing of hope within some of the participants, while also encountering the power of the concepts for myself. This experience, and my journey alongside several Rwandans, was instrumental in bringing the PDW into acceptance for wider use – and so extending its influence throughout Rwanda. I particularly noticed the impact of the workshop upon Josephine. Following is Josephine's account of her life when she came to the healing workshop.

> Since my childhood I have experienced several periods of oppression committed against the Tutsi ethnic group, culminating in the genocide of 1994. It's hard to fully express my feelings and my behaviour at the time I attended these workshops. I felt I had no life within, and many difficulties in relationships, especially with people who did not belong to my ethnic group.
>
> Despite the good education my parents gave me – and I am thankful that they taught me not to retaliate with harmful actions – nevertheless I suffered strong and painful anger within me. I lost peace and had a permanent headache.
>
> I hated myself and could not see any purpose in my life. I lived day to day, just like a child. If I tried to plan a little way ahead, I always failed and kept asking myself, "Why am I here, why am I here at this point now?" I always felt bitter. And my thoughts would cross normal, safe boundaries in the mind of a responsible parent. Sometimes I wished I possessed the power that could set alight the hills where they live.
>
> I would sit and dwell about the events of 1959: how my mother was beaten, of the bushes in which I slept before coming back home, and running away from school for six years. I

recalled the pit into which my father was thrown and from which he was able to escape. But my father-in-law and his sons died in 1963. I would remember the machetes and the sticks from which we escaped in 1973, the killings and the looting and the burning houses in 1993, and how we ran away. But eventually we returned home to wait for the fatal day when I was made an orphan, a widow and a person without any remaining roots.

Of the eleven siblings in my family, only three of us remain. My father and my mother were killed by machetes, as were more than fifty of their grandchildren. Nothing remains for future memories. I cannot even speak about hundreds of other close relatives who disappeared. In the families of my siblings, only my children escaped death – no other single relative was left alive. From this you can see the weight of sorrow and anger that I held in me because of these events.

In the bereavement workshop, after I wrote a letter of farewell to my baby brother, I glanced across the table at Josephine, who was writing, line after line, until she put down her pen and lay her head on the table. When we shared about our experience, Josephine said, "I wrote goodbye to my brother, goodbye to my uncle, goodbye to my niece, goodbye to my neighbours, goodbye to my friends and so on. When I reached fifty names, I stopped – not because I ran out of names – but because I was so exhausted by all the sadness."

The next workshop focused on bringing our hidden emotions out into the open – anger, fear and hate, as well as love, joy and hope. Josephine was adamant, "I can never go back to the spot where I saw my brother die . . . At the market, I hate seeing those people from the other ethnic group. I wish I could die. I am not sleeping well. Life has no meaning." This focus on feelings helped us understand our genuine natural selves in contrast to the expected behaviour of our parents, significant elders and the broader community.

One month later, as we began the session on forgiveness, Josephine surprised me by saying, "I went back to the house where my brother was killed . . . I was amazed. It was okay – the fear has lost its power over me." By facing her fears, her anger subsided and Josephine became more open and strong. This freed her to let go of her bitterness as well as the right to seek revenge. In the following narrative, she recounts the inner changes she experienced from the PDW.

The PDW enabled me to mourn the loss of my relatives, and I sincerely bereaved them. Prior to that I never understood how I could farewell deceased loved ones if I was not with their dead bodies. I learned how to do it, and after some time I felt relieved of strong inner feelings. The workshops were held in the daytime, and every night I thought deeply about my relatives – their loving good deeds, which I was missing, the gentle touches and their desire to strengthen me. I honoured their memory and thought of the plans they'd held for my future.

Because of these workshops, I've come to understand myself and the causes of my inappropriate behaviour. I gained the insights and strength to manage my anger. I understand that my life is worth caring for as long as I'm alive. I realize we will all die one day, but to die as a coward or because of despicable actions is the worst thing. And so I choose to continue my life in this world with all the human dignity I can muster.

A few weeks later, Nsabiyera, our PDW translator, said to me, "I just spoke to Josephine and she wants to find the neighbour who helped kill her brother." Josephine's account of what led up to this step reveals the courage that emerged in her through the workshop:

I've decided not to pay back in kind to the people who did wrong to my family, rather to help them as offenders [who have] come to realize the wrongness of their deeds and to invite them to change and reject such behaviour. With this in mind I tried to approach one family I knew well, and were part of the perpetrators of genocide, particularly in relation to the death of my brother. At my first chance of making contact with the man, he saw me approaching, feared for his life, and ran to hide in somebody's house. I was unable to trace him further on that occasion.

Days later, my children informed me that they had seen the children of this man. So I asked my children to find where this family was living, and a while later I met with the man's wife. I asked if she could take me to her home, but she looked fearful at the suggestion. I tried to show her that I did not intend to take revenge, and we chatted politely as I told her about my relatives who I lost.

This was a crucial moment for Josephine if she was to gain the confidence of the wife in the early stage of attempting to make contact with the husband. Josephine continued her story:

> We who remain need to live as human beings and use all of our wisdom to distinguish between right and wrong, good and bad. I discussed with her several examples of the disadvantages of bad deeds, such as were committed in Rwanda. I also assured her that I did not intend to take revenge because to do so would make me no different from the killers of my relatives. I said I felt pity on those people whose hearts are like wild animals.
>
> Slowly I observed a change in her, and she began to share with me the difficult life that their family had lived in the refugee camps, and how they returned in fear to live in Rwanda, and the kind of life they now lived. After some time, she began to ask me how my relatives, including my brother, died. When I explained to her how they were killed, she became sad and started to cry. She cursed the devil who deceived people to devour each other. She also apologized that she was unable to hide or protect any people at the time because it could have led to her own death. She shared other thoughts to indicate her deep sense of shame at what happened.
>
> In due course the woman told her husband about our conversation and convinced him that they both needed to visit me. When we met, we chatted for a long time. As he shared his side of the story, he talked repeatedly about the drawbacks of wrong behaviour.
>
> Then the couple started to relax with me, expressing their desire to be involved in activities that would help orphans and vulnerable survivors as a response to the losses to which they had contributed. If there weren't ongoing killings, which have been resurrecting ill feelings about ethnicity and hindering our further opening up, we would have already become true friends.

The PDW sessions on emotions introduced a way of communicating known as "*I'm OK, You're OK.*" This was the title of a popular book by Thomas Harris in 1967. Harris was a student of Dr Eric Berne who developed the concept of Transactional Analysis, which is a method of studying transactions between individuals. Josephine had absorbed the ideas from that concept and was

Conversation builds trust

putting them into practice, so the other woman was not intimidated by her words (You are OK) – and Josephine no longer feared that she would lapse into an irrational or uncontrolled outburst of anger (I am OK). Her sensitive response impressed the mother; this led to further openings to connect with her, and she eventually brought Josephine into conversation with the husband.

Insights from Josephine

Josephine's story highlights six key factors that have been central in the process leading to Rwandans' healing.

First, the PDW groups were small. All were composed of hurting people who were willing to share painful stories and hold others' stories within a safe place of confidentiality and mutual respect. As trust was nurtured, participants were free to feel their wounds, grieve their losses and better understand their pain. Healing began in this place of openness and safety.

Second, the cultural and family models in Rwanda encouraged people to ignore the pain of emotional wounds, put on a brave face and press on with life. Thus in everyday life, pain continued to rise up from the subconscious, affecting how people viewed themselves and related to others. The oft-quoted Rwandan saying, "The tears of a man flow down to his stomach," implies that tears should not be seen in public.

Misconceptions about pain and hurt are not confined to Rwanda. "Time heals all wounds" is a popular, yet misleading, belief in many cultures. The PDW, with its focus on healing, challenged the reliability of this statement, which was made in 160 BCE from Terentius Publius Afer. Beyond question Terentius was fortunate; as an African slave in France, his master recognized his skill as a dramatist and liberated him from servitude to follow his career. Terentius, also known as Terence, received justice and so had every reason to heal. But he was an exception, not the rule. About 250 years before Terence, Hippocrates noted, "Healing is a matter of time, but it is sometimes also a matter of opportunity." I learned the truth of this in Rwanda. While time does bring perspective, it does not heal painful inner wounds. Only healing heals.[5]

Third, most Rwandans did not have access to professional counselling, but with clear boundaries of safety, they did significant healing work in small

---

5. My source for the quotes by Terentius and Hippocrates is the fourteenth edition of John Bartlett, *Bartlett's Familiar Quotations* (New York: Little, Brown and Company, 1968).

groups. As discussed in Part 5: *Judging for Justice*, working through conflict in community has been an effective historical practice in Rwanda.

Fourth, the act of remembering difficult and painful experiences often re-opens wounds. Thus it is important to identify the feelings attached to these wounds: sadness, disappointment, betrayal, injustice, failure and fear. Forgiveness, which is about letting go, can only come after facing and mourning the painful emotions that grip us after experiences of grief and loss. Ndogoni, my psychologist colleague in Rwanda, emphasized this when he explained to me, "Without healing of our wounds, forgiveness is impossible."

Fifth, when we hold feelings inside our bodies, they impact our moods, relationships, choices and attitudes. By learning to take our feelings seriously, we can understand what actions specifically hurt us, and then we can choose a healthy response, rather than being trapped in unproductive patterns of wounding others out of our pain. When our spirit is wounded, our body pulls our energy inwards, seeking to protect us from further pain, whereas healing frees energy for other purposes, including reaching out to other people. When we begin to heal, we see the world in a different light. We can see those who hurt us and separate them from their actions. We can let go of some of the impact those actions had on us and allow those who hurt us to become human.

Sixth, although forgiveness may have no effect whatsoever on the person who did the wounding, it is crucial in the healing of the wounded person. As Lewis Smedes says, "Forgiveness sets a prisoner free, only to find the prisoner is me."[6] Forgiveness may seem to imply letting the other person 'off the hook' or ignoring the seriousness their actions. But forgiveness can include a call to restore justice and to live differently.

Because Josephine surrendered her bitterness and her 'right' to seek revenge upon those who killed her loved ones, she was able to speak the truth with gentleness, and talk about how those actions had affected her without blaming or shaming. She then asked those who hurt her to behave in a different way. Then she affirmed them in their desire to take responsibility for some of the consequences of their actions and to be involved in practical, caring actions for survivors. Following are Josephine's final reflections on the PDW:

> Thanks to the PDW I can truly say that I have moved from
> deep loneliness to be able to think properly, love my life, sleep

---

6. Smedes, *The Art of Forgiving*, 186.

with peace, remember my deceased relatives with joy, guide my children without becoming angry at them and so on. I no longer have a negative attitude towards Hutu, because I'm now able to hate a wrong deed done by a person, but not to hate a person because of their ethnic group. Before my healing I could not go to the Byumba market because I hated to see so many Hutu in the one place. Now I am fine when I go there.

Many of us in Rwanda are suffering unnecessarily because we lack knowledge of the healing process. We need those who can focus on building up people to recover and live again.

This list reflects so much of what I experienced in my own healing and transformation. What I particularly noted was the softening in me when I communicated difficult or sensitive matters to people with whom I formerly had difficulty in being open and honest. My change enabled me to state the truth as I saw it, but not in an accusing or belittling way.

Reaching out to the Edges

In time, many of the PDW participants became workshop leaders or small group facilitators, who then trained grassroots facilitators in the districts where they worked. Eventually, more than a thousand community volunteers were equipped to offer the PDW to local people. As the reach of the workshops extended, we could not keep track of all that had been, and continues to be, achieved. But scattered in urban and rural communities throughout Rwanda, there are leaders who have been trained to assist those who want to work through the unresolved pain of their past.

Professor Simon agreed to meet me for a final interview in 2012, after he returned from a month's healing work in eastern Congo. Weary and suffering from an infected leg, Simon greeted me with, "John, I need to go to the hospital, we only have

Professor Simon Gasibirege   © John Steward

an hour to talk." I asked him how his work had changed over the past fifteen years. He said, "People living far in the villages, and those not educated, tended to miss out on the opportunity to heal. Usually we worked with people living in or nearby towns and the educated in cities. I now try to go and reach more distant people."

I asked him to reflect on how the PDW had now expanded beyond his sphere of influence. He spoke first about his work in the prison at Butare:

> My experience in the prison was deep and interesting. In the beginning it was very difficult for my colleagues and me. The prisoners thought all those small group facilitators with me were Tutsi. And they thought, "This old man, who has been thirty years in exile and says he is concerned about us *genocidaires* (killers), can't be trusted." I told them, "We are here for you, because prisoners have a role in the re-construction of this country." They were passive during the first two days, waiting and wondering, "Can these Tutsis really help us?" As we began the third day, they said to us, "We wondered why you really came, but now we know you seek the best for us."
>
> After participating in the PDW, these same prisoners began a workshop for others in the prison. They developed their own syllabus and offered it to other prisoners. Many of them phoned me after their release and said, "Simon, we are out now, on early release, thank you for your help."

I asked Simon if he was concerned that many of the facilitators had not been trained as psychologists or trauma counsellors. He replied:

> Every facilitator needs to be compassionate; if you do not have compassion you cannot do the work. You need to understand that the people are in big trouble, they passed through a painful past and it is very important to understand their emotions by listening to them.
>
> . . . My emphasis is on the sharing of experiences. My goal is not to be a therapist – each member in the group is the therapist for the others. We involved others from the community, and not just the violated, so that the latter are not isolated, as that tends to produce stigma.
>
> . . . Communitarian health is based on my conviction that you can find people who are able to be a resource to help others in

any village, town and church and any local group or association of people. I came to realize that others could try. When you can try, you can do and have the courage to continue. It is very difficult at first, but after you've done it, you have trust in yourself and in your work. Now they do not need me because they can do it themselves. I went once or twice to observe the community facilitators and I'm happy with their work.

I asked him to talk about the process of freeing people to talk about shameful, private matters among peers. Simon replied:

Having rules is part of a proper process – so, for example, the rule: What is spoken here stays here (within the group). This commitment to confidentiality builds trust. Our 'Rules of Protection' ensure confidentiality. In our introductions, we greet one another, we smile and we look at the face of the person who is speaking. This helps to create an open environment. We use poems, as people respond to this, and it helps them to share. We also talk about how we were last night, and this creates bonds of trust. Above all, it is the one-on-one sharing which gives people the courage to open up.

power of poetry

I prefer the community-based approach because NGOs tend to gather people from various areas. Then, when the people go to their home districts, they are separated from each other. We keep alive the sense of closeness if we keep the work local. We can develop cooperatives; we can resolve conflicts as an outcome of having participated together. We can more easily do follow-up. Also the community offers the context and the focus for the workshop and they gain by bringing their own leadership to the event.

Having come to realize the stress in the PDW on how crucial emotional awareness is to forming good relationships, I asked Simon about the Rwandan tendency to dismiss or devalue emotions. He responded:

Emotions always have a context. Parenting is the basis of controlling emotions – parents school the emotions of their children. The media focuses on the bad side of emotions – pain, loss and suffering. Most of the time, emotions scare us, and we push them away. We cover them up and we don't fix them. So emotions keep on piling up within us.

Religious groups can play a big role in this problem. For example, the words, "Don't let the sun go down on your anger," may suggest that anger is bad, whereas the words are suggesting, "Face your anger now and don't let it stay with you into tomorrow." Many religious groups manipulate by working on the emotions, and also in politics and business. The psychology of marketing is often nothing more than emotional abuse.

We now work in Rwanda with released prisoners who are hurting and whose hearts are not ready to build good relationships. We find in working with couples that the husband might begin to threaten his wife, even in the workshop, but by dealing with their pain the relationship can become joyous.

Also we work with young couples, but in the context of the whole community. Parents talk to their children and share the information sheets that we provide. We do not do any gender-based work, because it always brings out problems that can't be solved as long as the other partner is not there. Our research is showing that the out-working of traumatization is no longer public – its effects are private. We see it with husbands not relating to their wives, women drinking, cheating between partners. Therefore we work on rebuilding families.

Finally, when I look at Rwanda today I see people drinking, eating, dancing, laughing, singing – and lots of physical construction, as if Rwandans have decided to come from death to life. I see a country at life. Speaking of the internal needs of people, some are getting well and developing well – even becoming prosperous. Others have lost hope and are really suffering. Finally, a lot of people in Rwanda are trying to find a way to recover.

As I left the interview, I was grateful to have met Simon, who had traversed his own healing journey in Belgium and returned to Rwanda to help his people after the genocide, using his own experience of healing to invite transformation in others. I reflected on my own decision to come to Rwanda because it was an opportunity for me to work in a difficult place, as I had told my friend who thought I was going abroad 'to wander'. Little did I know then how my experiences in this beautiful, broken country would continue to transform me.

I became an advocate of the PDW in Rwanda because of its suitability for Rwandans and its similarities to the healing process that had helped me in Australia. Just as my life had begun to change, I believed that more Rwandans would begin to change when they were ready to. Those who were willing became like fuel to the fires of hope burning in my heart. In Part 2: *Looking for the Light*, I introduce Karigirwa and Munyeli, whose dramatic stories led to wonderful healing in their lives and in Rwanda.

2

Looking for Light

"When you begin to articulate what the pain is about,
that is when you begin to heal."

Pumla Godobo-Madikizela

Nyamata

Nyamata is a township in the low-lying savannah bush country beyond the papyrus swamps of the Bugesera region, south of Kigali.[1] Long ago, this area was a refuge for exiled and marginalized Tutsi trying to survive among the wild animals that threatened them and their cattle. This is where the killings of Tutsi began in the early 1960s. The pale brown track between Nyamata and Kigali was filled with potholes, making the trip a nightmare slog in the rainy season and unpleasantly bumpy in the baking heat of the dry season.

The bridge spanning the Nyabarongo River, which passed through the swamps, was guarded by soldiers day and night, who demanded to see identity papers and passports. Once, the soldiers wanted to confiscate a video camera in our vehicle, but as they could not get it to work, they returned it. Yet when we reached Kigali, the camera worked perfectly, saving valuable footage of orphan children in Nyamata, which when shown raised funds to care for some of Rwanda's child survivors.

Driving towards Nyamata, we passed the Ntarama genocide memorial church, which held 5,000 bodies from the genocide, deaths that were horribly premeditated. In 1994 vulnerable moderate Hutu, as well as Tutsi, gathered there desperately seeking refuge within the fence of the Ntarama

---

1. Church, *Forgive Them*, 60–61.

Catholic Church compound. But the church gates were stormed by busloads of Hutu fighters brought in from the north, who then rampaged through every building in the compound, cruelly massacring everyone inside. Only a handful escaped.

In 1996 the forensic anthropologist Clea Koff experienced the site as an eloquent and complex space:

> Ntarama is a memorial but it is also proof. Proof of the stories from the genocide that are so often set against a backdrop of churches; proof that the killers couldn't be bothered to hide the evidence (arrogance? laziness?); proof of the systematic nature of the killing (people from disparate, rural areas were brought to collection places); and the scores of bleached bones on the platforms are proof that even those who escaped the church were killed outside and their bodies lay where they fell.[2]

In spite of the poverty and homelessness that plagued the survivors in Nyamata, and in its surrounds such as Ntarama, it was marked by the positive influence of healing workshops and community change. I made more visits to this township than anywhere else in Rwanda, drawn by its mix of light and darkness, despair and hope, pathos and exhilaration. One of Nyamata's moving forces was, and continues to be, Karigirwa.

Karigirwa

As with many middle-aged Rwandans, Karigirwa was born outside of Rwanda. I did not feel free relating to her because her preferred language was French. While she could barely communicate the basics in English, I couldn't speak any French, so we usually just exchanged a few words and smiled at each other.

Although Karigirwa participated in many of the mentoring and reflection sessions I facilitated for Rwanda's healers, she remained a distant figure for most of my time in Rwanda. Eventually, Karigirwa related her story with the help of a translator who, typical of many young educated Rwandans, was sufficiently fluent in English to translate the sophisticated nuances of *Kinyarwanda*.

---

2. Quotation from Clea Koff, *The Bone Woman*, (London: Hodder, 2004), 101, with permission from the author.

I was very interested to hear what Karigirwa would tell me as she shone a reflective light on her past:

> As a Rwandan family living as exiles in Burundi, we were poor. Our food came from our garden and by doing work for other people. Because my family's background was Rwandan, we were never accepted as Burundians, even though I was born there. I felt this discrimination at school, where the pass mark was set at 40 percent for Burundian children, but 70 percent for those of Rwandan origin. I was deeply hurt and impacted by the unfairness. So I never could be happy.
>
> In trying to cope with this, I went to live with my sister in Congo, but after four years of secondary school I was unable to finish my studies there. Since I failed to obtain my graduation certificate, I returned to Burundi and began work as a primary school teacher.

Both these countries educate in French, so Karigirwa was able to move between the two education systems, but the dislocation affected her, since she had to live far from her parents.

> After four years back in Burundi, I married and my life improved. But three years later, during the war, when Burundian President Daday died, rebels came and took my husband captive. We were Catholics, and our family hid in the house of a foreign priest. But this priest gave the key of his house to the killers, who used it to gain access. They took away my husband. My children and I spent four days there without eating, while we heard the priest having his regular meals. When one of my children asked for food, she was given a doll. I kept that doll for a long time, but the memories it brought made me cry.
>
> I was left alone with two small children, as the other members of my extended family in the community were also taken captive. After three days, some of them were executed – the men first, then the boys (to avoid revenge later in life) and then women. My children were two years old and five months old at that time, and I went looking for my husband, but could not find him. We were trapped, until a nun showed compassion and called Tutsi soldiers, who rescued us and took us to a camp.

> Then they put us in a taxi to Bujumburra, the capital of
> Burundi. People in the taxi unknowingly revealed that my
> husband had been killed. My husband was a doctor, who was well
> known where we lived, and these people boasted, "We killed and
> burned him," not realizing I was his wife. I desperately wanted to
> go and see the site where this happened and to talk to the locals
> about it, but I was unable to.
>
> Then rebels got into the vehicle, and they killed the nine
> others in the taxi by stoning them, but they did not kill me. And
> so I survived. Like it or not, I now faced a life of widowhood.

We paused to take a few deep breaths, sip our bottled water and mop our
brows. These breaks created space for Karigirwa's feelings to catch up with
her mind. Karigirwa continued, describing her return to Rwanda and the
struggle to make a home in a land where she had never lived.

> With my children, I spent a year in Bujumburra, and then we
> heard things were settling down in Rwanda, so came to Rwanda
> in 1994. On the trip into Rwanda, the car broke down and a
> Rwandan rebel militia group threatened us. In our vehicle were
> three families, plus my mother and a sibling. The militia were
> trying to kill us by smashing our heads together. Death seemed
> imminent, so I asked for a bottle of water. I prayed over it and
> baptized my children and one other child. I was told to say my
> last prayer before dying, but just then Burundian soldiers arrived
> and rescued us.
>
> After all these terrifying experiences, I arrived in Rwanda
> with deep wounds in my heart. I decided never to talk with a
> Hutu or even to greet them. When in mixed groups, I ignored the
> Hutus and did not even acknowledge their presence. I ignored all
> the maids and house helps who were Hutu. At times life was so
> difficult that I could not go to work for up to three days as I sat
> just weeping at the pain of it all.

Karigirwa was not alone in her struggle. Over a million other Rwandans had
returned from exile after the genocide and faced the challenge of clashing
emotions: the joy and hope of living in the motherland, the terror and hurt
they had suffered in long-term exile, grief over the loss of loved ones, the
chaos and confusion of daily life in a devastated Rwanda. Many of them

would eventually come to feel, "The ones who died are lucky. We have the misfortune of living in this mess with all its sorrow, loss and shame."

I looked back on my brief experience of dislocation in 1997 and realized how unsettled Karigirwa must have felt during her first year in Rwanda. Karigirwa continued:

> I had been back in Rwanda for a year and a half when I married again. I found it hard to accept my new husband, as I was constantly comparing him with my first husband. I felt deeply confused and guilty because, years before, my first husband had asked, "If ever I die, will you marry again?" I never answered that question. Now I was married to another man without being disconnected from my first husband.
>
> All the time, people around me were talking about what they went through in Rwanda in 1994 and before, so I had plenty of opportunities to consider my own terrible story and feel the weight of carrying all of the pain and the loss. I had so many unanswered questions in my mind and did not have the comfort of finding, farewelling and burying the body of my late husband. I was chained by my grief and self-doubt. Then in 1997, I was invited to attend the introductory day of Professor Simon's PDW. There I learned this workshop would be an important experience for me, because I would have an opportunity to open my heart in a safe and confidential environment. I was not disappointed.

In spite of our language barrier I had come to know Karigirwa as a woman of refinement, dignity, faith and natural leadership, who was committed in her work of trauma awareness and healing, and appreciated for her competence by her colleagues. She now explained four major impacts upon her from participating in the PDW.

> The first three-day workshop focused on bereavement. I had opportunity to face my grief and my loss and to write a letter of farewell to my first husband, as if I were writing it on the day before he died. I asked his forgiveness for not replying to his question. I even apologized for marrying again, explaining to him that I needed protection. Then I took the letter to my new husband and talked about it with him. Our relationship changed. Previously, I felt guilty in the presence of my second husband, but now I felt goosebumps when he came to interact with me. I

was able to accept him because of being detached from my first husband. This was the first impact for change in my life after 1994.

I had observed her husband, a gentle giant full of compassion; I could appreciate how his supportive presence gave strength to Karigirwa. She paused to give a deep sigh, expressing her relief, then continued:

> The second impact came when I stopped differentiating between people and their ethnicity. Until this time, I could not eat while Hutus ate at the same table, I only drank. Refusing to eat was my protest against them. Then I learned that it was important for me to separate those who were killers from other Hutu. I came to accept that each person is a human being and that those who killed have the option of seeking forgiveness.

Karigirwa often came across as cool and self-contained. I was keen to hear the impact of the PDW session on her emotions. She commented:

> With regard to my emotions, [I realized that when I was abusive towards others, I was also suffering myself.] This made me cry for days at a time. I learned how to talk appropriately and to control my feelings – to acknowledge to whom I am speaking, their circumstances and never to say anything that could hurt another person. This knowledge of how to speak in a manner called, "I am OK, you are OK," was the third impact of the healing workshops upon me.
>
> The fourth impact, which helped to change me, was grasping how to forgive. I learned to begin with forgiving myself, and then I could look at what to forgive in the actions of others. I came to value forgiveness. I asked forgiveness of my husband, my children, of other people in the community, my neighbours and colleagues. I was even able to ask forgiveness of those people whom I had refused to help or to acknowledge. Now I am able to live with other people in my area as if we are all one family.

It was, at first, uncanny to know how aspects of Karigirwa's story connected with my own experience of transformation. Despite my life being far less dramatic and troubled than hers, we both were able to resolve our issues of bereavement, emotional immaturity, non-judgemental relating and resentment. Later, as I considered these commonalities, I realized that these are widespread issues. We just don't have enough mentors and role models in these areas of the human condition.

The PDW for Children

With the help of some fellow graduates, Karigirwa brought the PDW home to people in Nyamata. After several workshop cycles for adults, she gathered some of the graduates and developed a working group to brainstorm the needs of school children and young people in the area. They collaborated with schoolteachers to identify children who showed signs of trauma. Then they adapted the workshop to their needs and ran them on weekends. Karigirwa described the program as "a form of group therapy that enables children to consider normal life problems. Some of the children missed their lost loved ones so badly. Children of those who committed genocide felt ashamed and it was hard for them to be unable to visit their fathers in distant prisons. Talking about that disappointment helped them to cope better."

In 2004, I learned more about Karigirwa's child focus when we drove along a narrow, sandy track to a remote area west of Nyamata. For sixteen kilometers, we wove between bushes, sometimes parting a grazing herd of cattle or goats, and passed through isolated settlements in order to meet Ndahimana and his parents. They explained how Ndahimana was having trouble sustaining regular attendance at school, as he had a phobia from birth, which he expressed as fear of people, especially those who gave orders and made demands. In 1992, while still in his mother's womb, Ndahimana's parents were confronted by local *interahamwe*, the youth arm of the Hutu power movement, who went on to play a key role in the genocide. Ndahimana's father told how they were beaten and violated in their own home. Then, as they fled in terror, one of the youth threw a rock, which hit the mother on the back. She collapsed, and the father picked her up in his arms and carried her into the bush to hide from further attack.

Ndahimana was born just a few months later, only to live through the horrors of 1994, when his parents often moved him from place to place to escape the killers. He was profoundly affected, so that at age seven, when boys begin school, he just ran home and hid. His father tried to talk with him, but could not hold his son's attention. A concerned teacher made a report to the PDW working group, and they invited Ndahimana to join with other children to process their problems.

psychological effect on development

Ndahimana attended six sessions, which he completed in July 2003. To the joy of his parents, he was able to sit with his dad and talk without any fear. When I visited six months later, he still had difficulty looking other adults in the face, but he could now play with other children, even taking a lead role in having fun with a group of boys. He was not yet ready for school and was still unable to accept requests from teachers.

Four years later, I visited the family again. They were excited to tell me how Ndahimana had advanced in confidence and would be attending a special boarding school. He remained in the room throughout my visit and smiled at me while I chatted with the family. He asked his dad to tell me, "I was so excited when I heard the *muzungu* was coming back to visit, I did not sleep for the past few nights."

When I asked if I could meet those who had assisted Ndahimana in his healing, I was taken to the provincial health centre in Nyamata, where I met several women graduates of the PDW – friends of Karigirwa who had been trained to identify signs of trauma in children. They were among the twenty volunteers in the area who had offered help to people with trauma, a group that included civil servants, teachers, nurses, administrators, health care workers and peasant farmers.

They explained how they had attended to their own healing, but were troubled by their many friends and neighbours whose emotional needs were not being met. So they borrowed a room in the health centre and completed training in counselling and the facilitation of healing in others. Several focused on responding to the needs of children. One of the schoolteachers introduced Ndahimana to them after he had run away.

At the time of my visit, this group had helped one hundred and six children and were about to run the program for fifty more. They worked in five clusters of ten children and two facilitators. They played games to relax before sharing their memories. Then they affirmed one another's hurt and confusion. They also shared about their recovery and learned new habits of survival and acceptable behaviour.

The group of leaders spoke proudly of how far they had come, noting that many in the community were recovering from their wounds. They also stressed how their healing had led them to invite others into the healing experience. This assistance had helped Ndahimana turn a corner in his life so that he could attend boarding school. This story represented an abundant fruit from Karigirwa's commitment to lead others along the path of healing and hope.

Karigirwa Looks Forward

When I last met Karigirwa in Nyamata, she greeted me in strong, clear English. After I expressed surprise, she smiled and explained, "Two of my children are studying in America. I have had to learn to speak English so I can visit them." I felt relief, because now we could communicate directly with each other for the first time. I had heard she'd been sick with cancer and was not expected to survive. But she had been through months of treatment, and as she sat before me, she looked remarkably fit and well. "It's a miracle," she explained.

Despite her long struggle with cancer, she had remained a woman of great energy, continuing to drink her daily dose of Red Bull, a caffeine-enriched drink. After catching up, Karigirwa reflected on her years of work in bringing healing to people affected by the genocide and exile:

> As a facilitator of the PDW, I worked with different groups of all ages – from widows to young children. Many have been impacted by their participation. Overall I facilitated more than 100 people each year for eleven years. The most challenging issue was one that continually arose: the psychological problems in people related to their material needs. When you can't solve the latter, it is very hard to work on the former. For example, one woman who was living in a tent found she was adversely affected every time that it rained. This problem became her pre-occupation – not healing from her trauma.

She spoke about how such group gatherings reflected hope for the Rwandan people and culture:

> The Rwandan culture is based on solidarity, and the PDW re-created this through the support experienced by each participant in the small group discussion. During the genocide, this kind of support was lost. In the process of burial, people would traditionally come together, but in 1994 there was no time to do that. The workshop was a way of providing interaction between people, which brought back the hope of life.
>
> The first step of the workshop is for participants to remember everything that happened and they recall what they could have done. They cry when they see what they have lost. This lessens their improper attachment to those who died and links them

more to their own life. For so long they have felt empty, and now they begin to look for something to fill the emptiness. They begin to see people who can fill the gaps, and they begin to meet others again. They begin to be invited to weddings. Many learn to celebrate life once more.

Karigirwa and her husband had hosted a young soldier who had returned from fighting to find his family killed. Realizing he had nowhere to stay and no one to be with, he began to struggle with his trauma.

He went back to school and for six years threw himself into his studies, taking no holidays. Then he came to stay with us. When he participated in the PDW, he talked about keeping his father's bones and how in order to be happy, he would need to brush them clean and smear them with oil. He would spend the whole night fighting with imaginary Hutus in his dreams. In one nightmare, he tried to grasp at his late mother and his sisters. These visions ceased after he participated in the PDW and he could begin to relate to people. But he said that he couldn't marry until he found his mother's bones. He wanted to be able to put them in a bag and bring her bones to the wedding. He tangibly improved and was able to have a girlfriend. At last contact, he went to Sudan with the UN peacekeeping force.

We spent some moments celebrating Karigirwa's contribution in having an impact on one thousand one hundred people through her work. We wondered together how many others these transformed healers had influenced in turn. Then Karigirwa explained how she had moved from running healing workshops for groups to mentoring and counselling individuals. Also she had opened a centre for training and accommodation as well as a wedding planning business and offered to give me a tour of her new work.

First, we looked at the impressive centre she and her husband were running for tour groups, workshops, weddings, ceremonial events and other public programs. Then she introduced me to the way she was using her entrepreneurial skills to arrange weddings, including preparing the ceremony, clothing, facilities, decorations, content and course of the program. Both the centre and the weddings were community-focused ways of bringing together local involvement, as weddings restored life and brightness to communities, and training offered new skills and time for reflection.

During my visit, Karigirwa ran five weddings in two days – two in Kigali and three in the vicinity of Nyamata. Her energy and creativity took my breath away. On the Saturday, I was an unscheduled guest at one of the weddings. Held outside, under grey, threatening skies, the families of the bride and groom sat opposite each other under two impressive white marquees with coloured banners. All the interactions of the wedding took place in the open, ten-meter space between the families.

Karigirwa played her 'mother-hen' role brilliantly: seeing the bride was properly dressed and ready, getting her into position at the right moment and prompting the bride and groom in their words as the ceremony proceeded. The wedding guests and the crowd of several hundred loved the two comedians, who were dressed as shepherds, humorously bantering about the bride and groom in farming terms: wishing them "green pastures, flocks of little ones, productive lives," etc. It was a great time of celebration and laughter.

Traditionally, the exchange of liquids between two parties in Rwanda was a way of celebrating agreement, acceptance or contracts. As this segment took place between the parents and representatives of the bride and groom, I noticed the ceremonial drinking of sorghum or banana wine through long bamboo straws in a clay pot had been updated for this ceremony with a more informal rite – the exchange of large bottles of Coca-Cola and plastic straws. This change reflected a modern response to the growing concern in Rwanda around the tendency of some to drown painful memories using alcoholic drinks.

Bordering the open, grassed area, on the edge of the road, children stood four and five deep. Several times, they moved back to allow a laden truck to grind its way along the track in front of them. I was struck by the children's energy, smiles, health and improved standard of clothing, in comparison with my previous visits to the area, reminding me of Karigirwa's reflections about her work with children.

With the wedding formalities over, Karigirwa drove me to the border of Rwanda and Burundi, where staff showed me around the offices for border control. I recalled earlier stops I had made at posts like this, where an hour delay was normal. Two staff members proudly explained they had reduced the waiting time for obtaining permits to ten minutes – a sign of the general improvement in Rwandan standards of efficiency. We turned towards Nyamata, and Karigirwa made a final summary about the impact of the PDW in Nyamata:

I saw how many who couldn't be with Hutus were able to do that after their healing. Parents who had threatened their children (due to internalized anger) began to apologize for that. People who wouldn't cooperate with each other began to relate well. One wife wrote us a thank you letter saying, "You helped my husband, and now I am like a newly married woman: we share everything." On many occasions, those who had completed the PDW would ask us, "Can I bring my husband or wife or neighbour or a child or friend to get this help at the next course?"

As we drove, we passed a line of fifteen freshly constructed houses with cement walls and shiny tin roofs. Karigirwa told me that the government had built these *Imi-du-gu-du* – small colonies of houses neatly arranged in rows – for the latest returnees from Tanzania. We wondered why they had taken longer than most exiles to return.

That night I reflected with thanksgiving for how this widow, wife and mother had recovered from personal loss and deep trauma, then battled with cancer while she led more than one thousand one hundred others through their healing journeys. In the process, she had never lost her faith, her belief in herself, nor her commitment to use her energy to serve family, community and country.

Before leaving Nyamata, I asked Karigirwa how her views of the Catholic Church had shifted over these years and whether she felt bitterness towards the priest who failed to protect her first husband and to feed her and her children. She said that after the changes in her life through the PDW, she had thrown away the doll the priest in Burundi had given to her daughter, which brought Karigirwa great relief. She added, "I was able to forgive the Catholic Church and my children still go there. It was not the church that failed, but individuals in the church. My husband and I now attend a local Protestant church."

Karigirwa   © John Steward

The Confusing Role of the Catholic Church

Like Karigirwa, many Rwandans changed denominational allegiances after the genocide because of the failure of some priests and lay leaders to protect their parishioners. Because of Rwanda's Belgian colonial history and the work of Catholic missionaries, roughly two-thirds of Rwandans are Catholic – making it the most Catholic of all African countries. Historically, the ebb and flow of the bias of Catholic Church leadership in Rwanda reflected the movements of power and ethnicity in the society at large.

When I arrived in Rwanda in 1997, many survivors were expressing consternation regarding the failure of Pope John Paul II to apologize for the role of the Catholic Church in the genocide.[3] The Vatican was arguing that the genocide did not occur because of official church doctrines, but rather because of individuals' actions. While this was somewhat true, the Catholic Archbishop of Rwanda was a prominent member of the ruling party and served on the President's central planning committee until 1990, when he stepped down just before the Pope's visit to Rwanda that year. Until 1994, he retained a direct phone line to President Habyarimana and was a confidante of the President's wife. Many Rwandans believed that Catholics with access to government powers must have been aware that something serious was going to happen in 1994.[4] Yet few individual priests, bishops and church leaders in the country questioned the direction and ambition of military and civil leaders at this time.

Twenty-eight priests and some Protestant church leaders were on the list of those indicted with planning or being actively involved in the genocide. Some of these leaders cooperated with the killings by betraying the Tutsi in their congregations to the killers in order to save themselves or their ethnic group, putting ethnicity above the unity of the faithful. Some priests and bishops fled the country and received sanctuary in other African states, Europe and North America. Even though some Catholic churches, such as the ones at Nyamata and Ntarama, lost their status as a refuge when thousands died within the walls of cathedrals and church compounds, most of the deaths within church property occurred because proponents of the

---

3. The Pope did act to swiftly denounce the massacres as 'genocide' on April 10, 1994.

4. I also learned later that the Catholic Archbishop, two bishops and some priests were held under house arrest in Kabgayi and were subsequently killed by the soldiers who were guarding them.

genocide gave incentives to youth militia to slaughter people wherever they were gathering en masse.

While Protestants made up less than 20 percent of the population in 1994 and had a less conspicuous involvement, they, too, offered some well-known exceptions, particularly among Anglicans, Baptists, Presbyterians and Seventh-day Adventists. Muslims are said by some to have had the best record of non-involvement and earned a reputation for protecting vulnerable people, including some Christians.

As I searched for insight about the role of the church in the genocide, I learned that 25 percent of the Catholic priests in Rwanda perished during the genocide. When the killers gave the order, "Send the Hutu outside," ninety-five priests and over a hundred members of religious orders refused to divide their congregations along ethnic lines. Knowing they would die alongside their congregations in consequence of their refusal to cooperate, they responded with dignity: "On behalf of my congregation, there are neither Hutu nor Tutsi here. We are all Rwandans." Their martyrdom is a modern example of honourable and courageous sacrifice.[5] In summary, many Catholics suffered, some survived, others 'sold out' and a few became saints.

The Church Loses a Saint

At age 75, Mr Iyamuremye Saulve was known for his humility, love for others and skill in crafting songs, composing and playing music. He, his wife, four sons and two daughters were with hundreds of others, seeking shelter from the killings in western Rwanda within their local Catholic Church. In that place of hoped-for refuge, local militia, who forced their way in, cruelly massacred them.

Amazingly one young lad survived the carnage when he fell under the crush of bodies and later fled when nightfall came. He recalled what he heard and saw:

> Saulve, a Tutsi, was the target of the *interahamwe* [militia]. When it was time to kill him, all the local killers refused. They said, "We cannot kill such a holy man." And they told those who gave them orders, "You go and kill him yourself. We cannot touch this

---

5. Such martyrdom ranks alongside the killing of the Jesuit martyr St Paul Miki, one of twenty-six Christians crucified near Nagasaki, Japan in 1597.

man who we consider to be like our father." Three times the ones ordered to act refused.

Then their superior commanded them to find policemen from far away who did not know the man. They came to do the job, but before killing him these police said, "*Mzee* [old man], we are coming to kill you, but first we ask you to forgive us. We don't know you, we have never seen you, but we hear you are a good person. You have so much respect in this community, but we are following orders, so please forgive us. Because you are a good man, we will not kill you with a machete, we will not kill you with a spear. We will shoot you."[6]

He replied, "Before you kill me, can I talk to my wife for the last time?" They agreed, and the couple chatted, each apologizing to the other; they told each other what they needed to say and made their farewells. After, Saulve said, "Now we are ready, you can kill us." He was in the church, seated at his organ, because he had been singing and praying with all the church members sheltering there.

People were gathered at the parish from three communities and when they shot him, it was a signal that all the other people present could now be killed. . . . He was the only one shot by the police . . . the rest were killed by the local militia with traditional tools and machetes. It was very bad. People were cut into pieces and tortured. But he died peacefully.

Munyeli[7]

Munyeli told me this story of the dignified death of her father, Iyamuremye Saulve. She was with her two boys in Kigali when her parents and family died. Hearing the news, she went to bury them, but could only find the remains of one brother. Because so many bodies had been piled into pit latrines, no one could separate one person's remains from the others. Munyeli explained how fortunate she was to discover an eyewitness to the horrible events that took place:

---

6. During the genocide, most of the killings were with inefficient, hand-held traditional weapons that required brute force. People being targeted sometimes begged to be shot, and others even offered to pay for the 'privilege' of a quick end to their lives.

7. Munyeli is also known as Josephine. She is not the same person as the Josephine who is introduced on page 23.

When we buried the remains of the people who died in the church, I asked if there were any witnesses of the massacre. A young man survived, hidden under the bodies, which fell on top of him. He told me the whole story of how the people were killed. Without him I would not know of the grace and dignity, which my father demonstrated in the final moments of his life.

In 1992, Munyeli's husband had died unexpectedly while working in Italy, and she had returned to live in Kigali with their two small boys. Things had been tense in Rwanda since 1990, and some months before the genocide commenced, Munyeli was held captive at the roadside by an abusive group of young Hutu men. Suddenly a passing army major intervened to rescue her.

Later, she became reacquainted with one young man, when he offered to carry her groceries home for her and she paid him for his help. After one of several similar interactions, he revealed himself as the leader of the group who had threatened her. Once she got to know him, she began to confront him that not all Tutsis were bad. She even offered to pay for a coffin when his sister died. Munyeli also explained prejudice to him and challenged him to change his ways before it was too late. He visited her several more times to discuss leaving the militia and getting a job, but the genocide began before he could find work.

Munyeli described how this young man had visited her on the day the genocide began in Kigali:

> Early on the morning of 7 April 1994 someone knocked at the front gate of my house and the guard said, "Your *interahamwe* friend is here. Can I let him in?" I replied, "Maybe he's coming to finish all of us, yes – please open." When he entered, he shocked me. He looked terrible with his red eyes, wearing grenades all over his front, while brandishing a knife dripping with blood. He and his group had killed all night long. Yet he said, "Mama, has anybody come to harm you?" I said, "No, but I am afraid they might."
>
> He said, "Do not worry, nobody is coming to kill you, but if they do happen to put you on the list, I will come and try to rescue you and the boys. Nothing bad will happen to you." And then he read me the lists of people who were to be targeted in my neighbourhood. He said, "We will start with this man. He's tough, he's arrogant, and he's a big Tutsi." Afterwards I thought,

"Those people shouldn't die. Better, if they have to die, they die with us . . ." My sister who was living with me did not trust the words of this man and she left my house to seek safety elsewhere.

Munyeli took steps to bring all the vulnerable people in her street under the protection of her roof, and they bluffed and survived until the night the liberating forces of the Rwanda Patriotic Front (RPF) secured their area and took them to safety. She was transferred to the refugee camp in Byumba, from where she was offered a job in Uganda, which enabled her boys to continue their schooling.

During our conversation, she reminisced about how she was affected by these dramatic experiences, which challenged her as she strived for survival and faced an uncertain future.

> During the genocide when people were being killed, I really didn't know if I was afraid or sad. I was numb. I couldn't feel anything; I couldn't cry . . . I was like a tree, just standing there. I was afraid, but I did not let it stop me. I did what I could.
>
> Once we were safe in the camp in Byumba, I felt sadness, because of not knowing the fate of my other sister in Kigali. We kept looking for her among the casualties who arrived for treatment. Everyone in the camp waited to see if their relatives would arrive. But my sister did not come.
>
> How I cried when I learned she did not survive. Later on my way to work, I cried the whole way for my sister. I replayed the memory of her wedding in my mind. I cried, when I realized that I was one of only four in my family who lived. That was a huge loss and made me feel very sad.

These experiences gave Munyeli the desire to participate in the same PDW as Karigirwa. She told me how important this event was for her:

> The PDW transformed my life . . . My husband died when I was twenty-nine. I'd had no opportunity to revisit my story, what with the additional pain and pressure of raising my two boys on my own; then surviving many vulnerable moments before and during the genocide; and after that I grieved the loss of my kin. I was really broken.
>
> Participating in the PDW gave me opportunity to commence healing from those things. As I became more involved my pain diminished and hope returned. Now I have a story to tell

about healing and reconciliation. I deal with people's wounds because I believe healing is the foundation for reconciliation. Church leaders tell us to "forgive and forget", but if you *have* to forgive, then it is an obligation. It's like a mask. Forgiveness is a long process.

The PDW Spreads its Wings

Munyeli   © Dave Fullerton

Munyeli deserves much of the credit for expanding the work of the PDW. For several years after joining my team, she coordinated and administered the PDW program for Rwandan NGO staff and its spread into communities. With funding from several western countries, she inspired groups and individuals to participate and to take the opportunity to begin their healing under her committed leadership. As a result, the PDW became a resource for change in many communities. Munyeli's work with the PDW also prepared her for her later work in bringing thousands of accused Rwandans to justice, which will be discussed in Part 5: *Judging for Justice*.

The PDW was a tangible sign of hope for change in Rwanda, as it was a locally developed workshop that made significant differences in the lives of individuals. Earlier in the Prologue, I introduced the story of Drusilla, whose transformation began during a PDW and inspired me to believe that change could come to Rwanda through those who had the courage to face their fears and open their hearts in a safe, supportive context.

Hope for Healing the Church

When the genocide in Rwanda began in 1994, 80–85 percent of the population attended church. After 1994 the percentage remained almost the same. While it was a challenging time some Rwandans told me "we lost everything except our faith in God." During my first weeks in Rwanda, I received countless visits from church group representatives asking for help among faith groups.

Most of their proposals were to replace lost equipment or vehicles or to stage public events that had doubtful relevance to a traumatized and divided nation. Of those who petitioned for money, I found few who were willing to acknowledge their own need for healing. Though they were obviously suffering from trauma and stress, pride of position made it hard for many to accept their need for healing.

I wondered how these leaders could ever hope to become better leaders of their organizations and church groups – not to mention better spouses, fathers, brothers, uncles to their families and kin – if they did not receive healing themselves. Providentially, I met Dr Rhiannon Lloyd, a dynamic Welsh woman, and Nyamutera, a young Rwandan teacher. In Part 3: *Taming the Trauma*, we hear of Nyamutera's harrowing experiences and discover how Dr Lloyd's practical and positive approach assisted him and many other people, thereby impacting on the struggling church in post-genocide Rwanda.

3

Taming the Trauma

"The healing that is ours and nature's will come if we are willing,
if we are patient, if we know the way, if we will do the work."
Wendell Berry

Healing Wounds of Ethnic Conflict

After three months of familiarizing myself with the Rwandan context and background, I began to develop a strategy for reconciliation. The strategy included Professor Simon's "Personal Development Workshop" for those front-line workers who could get the time to participate in an eleven-day event. Then I followed up a contact Sandi had discovered in South Africa prior to our arrival in Rwanda, which led me to a "Healing the Wounds of Ethnic Conflict" (HWEC) workshop, which integrated Christian teaching with psychological theory.

The workshop founder, Welsh psychiatrist Dr Rhiannon Lloyd, had been deeply hurt as a young woman by Britain's lack of respect for traditional Welsh language and culture. The more bitter she became towards the British, the more she discovered that her anger was 'eating away' at her well-being. By following insights from her psychiatric training and Christian faith, she confronted these negative forces within and gradually gained release from her bitterness. She felt confident that the principles she'd learned could help others in situations of hurt, discrimination and injustice.

In 1995, a Dutch NGO in Nyamata hired Dr Lloyd to develop and test a three-day healing workshop that focused on influential Rwandan faith leaders and lay workers at the local level. When I entered Rwanda, the two-year experiment was complete, and I had heard that it might be suitable for church leaders and volunteer organizations. Yet even though the Dutch relief agency recognized the workshop's relevance to Rwandans, they had decided the work was not in their organization's long-term mandate.

At an informal meeting, Rhiannon explained to me that the workshop could not continue without financial assistance. I responded that I would not make any speedy decisions about funding, as I needed to know much more about the workshop and how it contributed to changing people in healthy, African ways. I asked her to submit a funding proposal for the HWEC workshop based on the development and testing period. I asked for participant evaluations, along with the workshop facilitators' reflections about its potential impact on Rwandans, including details about future plans and projected costs.

I set the bar high because in my first three months of exploring and learning, many other groups asked for funding without providing this kind of information. But when the HWEC proposal was submitted, I found it to be thorough and impressive. It included comments from previous participants of the workshop that indicated changes in beliefs, attitudes and behaviour.

> A pastor apologising on behalf of fellow Hutus: "We are sorry for the genocide. We hated you, we mistreated you, we killed your families, and we wounded you. We are sorry."

* * *

> One participant wrote: ". . . I found myself repenting of the sins which the Hutus have committed in killing many Tutsis. Eventually I found peace."

* * *

> Another participant said: "Three of my children died, one after another we buried them in a forest near the church. I was afraid to visit that burial site – even to look there. [After] the seminar everybody offered to go with me to the grave site."

* * *

> An angry Hutu described his change: "I am a Hutu. But I hated Hutus. They killed my father in 1959 . . . In 1994, they killed my two educated brothers in Kigali. I became more resentful and angry against my fellow Hutus. When . . . we fled to Tanzania

... I hid nearly 1,000 Tutsis in my church. My fellow Hutus were mocking me ... I only came back in December 1996. The people I hid welcomed me. After the workshop, I got delivered from my resentment and anger."

* * *

A Tutsi wrote: "Since my childhood I was taught to consider all Hutus as enemies. I hated them with all my energy ... My grandfather nourished my hatred with many stories of awful things Hutus did in 1959, causing our exile. I only regretted that I was a weak little girl who could do nothing to take revenge. When we came back to Rwanda in 1994, I was at the height of my hatred ... But when one of the workshop facilitators repented on behalf of the Hutus, I felt my heart broken. I felt love flowing in me."

This feedback suggested signs of transformation in Rwandans. The proposal also described how Dr Lloyd, her American assistant, and their Rwandan translator had reflected on two years of feedback and progressively adjusted the approach of the HWEC to ensure its appropriateness to Rwandan culture and history. Psychological concepts were connected to practical teaching about the down-to-earth need of rebuilding lives, restoring relationships and purposeful living. The workshop included ritual elements such as using a wooden cross as a symbol of suffering, writing pains on paper as a way of externalizing trapped emotions, nailing the papers to the cross to suggest sharing one's struggles with the divine, removing and burning the sheets to ensure confidentiality, while simultaneously releasing the hurt to the heavens. These solemn and profound rituals appealed to the Rwandan connection to the mystical and symbolic.

Since the workshop was only three days duration, it attracted busy clergy and lay leaders who could not make time for longer programs such as the PDW.[1] Yet it was interactive and involved small group conversations, where participants built trust and shared their painful experiences. This was an

---

1. In due course, the duration of the HWEC program expanded as the Rwandans on the team found it important to arrange follow-up gatherings in local areas. When the participants of the 3-day workshop returned to their communities and began to assist others struggling with consequences of the genocide they were overwhelmed. They needed equipping to face issues such as trauma and bereavement, widows who were raped, people troubled by memories associated with specific locations, recurring dreams, the fate of families, practical needs, etc.

initial step towards personal inner healing. Upon returning home, many of the participants multiplied the work of building trust and extending healing among members of their congregations and communities. The first HWEC I attended included a young participant named Nyamutera. After Rhiannon observed him she pointed out his natural leadership skills to me. She believed he had the potential to play a role in extending the reach of the HWEC workshops throughout Rwanda.

I was fortunate to watch Nyamutera's progress from a young adult to a mature man, from a Hutu who hated Tutsis to one putting his heart and soul into the work of reconciliation in Rwanda – and eventually to other countries in Africa and beyond.

Nyamutera

In summarizing his journey, Nyamutera traced the roots of his ethnic prejudice to several diverse influences:

> My research into my past revealed that my paternal grandpa was given to serve a Tutsi young prince. Because the prince was young, my grandpa – though he was Hutu – almost ruled for him. He had Hutu slaves himself. He was the prince's favourite and received land and cows from his boss. In the end, his noble manner became so Tutsi-like that in 1959, when the Tutsi monarch was overthrown, my grandpa had to flee because other Hutu, who considered him to be a traitor, hunted him. My grandpa later returned, dispossessed of his lands and cows. He grew up with bitterness, a Hutu hating the Hutu.
>
> I got the poison of prejudice against the Tutsis when I was eighteen, as other boys updated me with their version of the past. "The Tutsi are imperialist. They forced us to carry them on our backs, to work for them. They despized us, called us stupid. They were the masters and we their slaves." Though my Hutu grandpa benefited from the forced hard labour, I started to believe that 'we' had been cheated.
>
> The boys also taunted, "Their females are lazy and immoral. You never get a child because they sleep with their own brother when they want a baby. They will dismiss your family and bring in their relatives to enjoy the work of your hands." I think, now,

many Hutu ladies spread this rumour because of their jealousy, for it was also believed Tutsi ladies were more beautiful physically than their Hutu counterparts. This terrible poison affected the choice of female friendship for many a young man.

Nyamutera's honesty was refreshing, as was his insight into the confusing tension he felt between his beliefs and actions. He explained how the unquestioning prejudice that surrounded him sometimes led him to behave in ways that contradicted his Christian beliefs.

Before the genocide, most Rwandan Christians never learned there was anything wrong in thinking negatively about the other ethnic groups. In 1990, after all attempts failed to arrange peaceful repatriation of Rwanda's exiles, and the Tutsi-led army forced their way back into the north of the country, the war began. The old demon of fear expressed as, "They will come back to lord it over us," was a normal reaction for many Hutus, including Christians, who prayed fervently that God would 'deal with the enemy'.

I was confused. One day, like everyone else, I prayed against the return of the Tutsi from exile. The next day, I refused to celebrate with others when a prominent Tutsi commander died on the frontline. My understanding of Christian love for everybody, and my family upbringing, sometimes helped me stand firm in the turmoil of the war and the hatred propaganda in the media. But I confused everybody, including myself. I even found myself wondering, "What will happen if God gives me a Tutsi wife? What if everything they tell me about them is true?"

A Tutsi brother recently reminded me about one Sunday in 1993, when I shocked the congregation by asking them to "Stop calling the Tutsi RPF soldiers 'cockroaches', because one day God will bring them back to their nation. We will hug brothers and sisters in Christ among them. Some of them will join our choirs, and some will speak and lead us."

But the next day, when the radio reported a Hutu group were killed in an ambush, I returned to my prejudices and cursed the 'enemy' without even thinking about it. I was in this state of total confusion when I heard the news report on the evening of 6

April 1994, "They killed our President – if we Hutu don't defend ourselves they will kill us all."

This sense of bewildering confusion predominated in Rwandan culture for several years after the genocide, when everything seemed to be in flux. Some wanted to divide Rwanda into two separate states – one for Hutu and one for Tutsi. Others wanted to annex land from Congo to enlarge Rwanda and reduce pressure on the land.

Though Nyamutera's personal confusion challenged him, he took a stand and made difficult choices between choosing safety for a member of his family or living with regret. He continues:

Through the heat of the lead-up to the genocide, I knew that many young people just needed an excuse, because many were already armed and intoxicated to the full. I imagined that some Tutsi would be killed, but nothing like the extent of what happened. The 'landmine' of strong prejudice combined with political propaganda took [Hutu] onto the streets in mobs, in collective fear and hatred to kill man, woman, children in an unmatched creativity of cruelty.

I knew some young Hutu killed because they liked it. Other Hutu were forced to follow suit, some were even threatened with paying with their lives if they refused to kill. I did not want to be one of those caught up in the collective madness and chose to hide, even though I was not being hunted. Some Hutu were killed for carrying out acts of heroism by helping Tutsi friends hide or escape or for merely providing them with food. Things became complicated for me soon after the radio announced, "Whoever hides a Tutsi will be killed as an accomplice." I faced one of the greatest challenges of my life, when my brother told me, "Diane was thrown in the mass grave among many corpses, left for dead, with many machete wounds. She is hiding in our banana plantation. What do we do with her?"

Diane, our cousin, is almost two metres tall, a typical Tutsi, one you cannot pretend is a distant cousin. I had a choice, either to betray Diane and die in shame and regret, or to welcome her home and wait to die together. At this stage there was no indication of when the massacres would come to an end. There was no question of letting down Diane. My wife and I were living with my parents and they also had to accept the risk of dying. I was grateful when both my father and mum agreed.

My brother waited until dark to bring in Diane. She was emotionally paralyzed. My mum and wife, who are good with traditional medicines, used all kinds of leaves to treat her wounds until she regained her spirits. We cared for her until we found a friend who smuggled her over the western border to Goma, evading bloodthirsty militia patrols. Diane recovered and is now a beautiful mum to three wonderful kids.

Nyamutera traced his family's flight from Rwanda in 1994 as part of the mass movement into Congo of hundreds of thousands of (mostly) Hutus, and the trauma they experienced in the pressure of living in the refugee camps in Congo alongside promoters and activists of the genocide. He ruefully reported:

As my father prophesied, the unthinkable happened when the tiny Tutsi-led army received wings from the God of justice to win battle after battle. When my hometown fell into their hands in July 1994, the hate propaganda turned into a cry to "Flee from the cruel cockroaches that will kill any Hutu in their way." General fear pushed all of my family to join the hundreds of thousands fleeing across the border into the horrors of Congo.

Cholera welcomed us to the camps, and many of my family died. After the bodies of my father, my firstborn son, my sister and tens of thousands of other men and women were piled up like logs of wood and taken to mass graves to be dumped like rubbish, the guilt and shame of belonging to a tribe of mass murderers on the run, who were trying to escape justice, was replaced by anger and finger-pointing in accusation against God and Tutsis.

When life started to stabilize, we found refuge in the biggest camp in Goma, with one million people. Killers and innocent refugees were crowded together. Crime was high among those who would not share the aid fairly. Some young people, feeling extremely powerful with their weapons, simply decided to take whatever they wanted from the defenceless. Women paid a huge price, as rape became commonplace. Some women chose to 'seek protection' from less wicked guys so they wouldn't become prey for the bandits.

Congolese soldiers made it even worse by partnering with the militia in dispossessing people. The strongest controlled the stocks of food aid from the UN. The rest had to buy from them. It was a lawless jungle, where we prayed for protection in our plastic tents and meant it. It was not a religious rite, but a desperate plea to a higher power. Sometimes we prayed for rain just to have some water. Then we remembered that many in the camp were still sleeping under the moon, without any shelter at all. How confusing it must have been for God – with our prayers for water, while others prayed for the rain to stay away!

In spite of the chaos and challenges of life in the refugee camp, Nyamutera found some solace for his struggling life. He reflected:

I do not regret the two years I spent in the camp. I learned to trust God in all situations. Things became more stable with the take-over of the camp by UN soldiers. This led to more organized food distribution and accessible health posts. We felt blessed to have enough food to share with the poorest members of our congregation. I got a paid job, which led to foreign friends from many nations.

Yet the ongoing question among the refugees was, "How will the precarious situation in Rwanda come to an end?" and "What do we do next?" Nyamutera recalled the turmoil of his fellow Rwandans in the camps:

Some were so tired of the life and chose to risk a return to Rwanda, despite the continuous menacing propaganda that the new regime would kill whoever went back. Youth, recruited by the former Hutu army commanders, started militia training in the camp, envisaging they could fight their way back. Then Rwandan Vice President, Paul Kagame, threatened to dismantle the refugee camps.

After failing in an attempt to move to Kenya, Nyamutera and his family decided that whenever the opportunity came their way, they would leave the camp and return to Rwanda. In October 1996 RPF troops did invade eastern Congo, decimated the leadership in the camps and demolished the camp. Those who had no blood on their hands, or nothing to hide, made their way back to Rwanda. The others stayed on in Congo and went into the cities and forests, either not wanting to 'face the music' in Rwanda or wanting to continue the work of the genocide.

Once back in Rwanda, Nyamutera and his family were in constant danger, because the country was neither stable nor at peace. In returning, he describes how he and his family were discriminated against:

> Though the government did its best to guarantee our safety and to make us feel welcome, my brother was kidnapped and killed by some angry returnees who could not distinguish between militia and innocent persons.
>
> The church was not very encouraging to us either, because returnees among long-exiled Tutsi, from Congo and Burundi, couldn't differentiate between militia and ordinary Hutu. To them, we were all coloured with the same brush.
>
> The attempts of Hutu militia to take control of the Northern part of Rwanda in 1997–1998 only exacerbated the tensions and suspicion. "Keep us alive, Lord," became our daily prayer. Our strong conviction was that our time was over. There seemed to be no future, no blessing or life at all for returnees like us. All of us were so discouraged that we could not envisage any future for us in Rwanda.
>
> When I made a job application to a Christian organization, the *muzungu* (foreigner) told me someone on her staff advised her not to take returnees if she didn't want to get into trouble. At that stage I had no idea of what a wounded heart could produce.

Then one day Nyamutera joined some volunteers at his church and unwittingly became involved in a HWEC workshop, which he now describes:

> My intention was to help clean the dormitories for the participants attending "a seminar on trauma healing." As the attendance was low, I was invited to occupy a seat to encourage the *muzungu* leader and her Tutsi interpreter. I sat, barely interested in what this little British lady was saying. At first sight, her stature did not in the least impress me. I immediately 'knew' that this event was a charade. Either it was to please the government, or she was there to spy on the Hutus who had returned from the camps. I simply decided not to fall into the trap. I was the only participant who understood English, but the tall Tutsi guy was not aware of that.

This Tutsi interpreter was a returnee from Uganda named Sabamungu, who eventually became co-leader of the workshop with Nyamutera. At the end of this part, I trace Sabamungu's narrative. In the next section, Nyamutera describes how he was drawn into the workshop in spite of his belief that it was a charade or a deception.

> My attention rose when some aggressive Hutus shared their suffering at the hands of bitter Tutsi genocide survivors. I was shocked to hear the interpreter translating literally for the foreigner some bad things that the Tutsis did to these Hutu. I wondered how he could 'betray' his ethnic group by telling all the truth that these people were bringing to light. I wondered why he didn't lie or change the facts, since he didn't have to fear being understood by the participants.
>
> This was the beginning of a long journey for me. My world of prejudice was shaken from the foundation for, I thought, "If this Tutsi can be honest and not hypocritical, maybe there are others who are like that – perhaps hundreds of them, even thousands." The most interesting part of the workshop was about likening God to a father. This had nothing to do with ethnicity, and I received much healing and was able to forgive a father who did not easily show us his love..

After forgiving his own father, Nyamutera recalled how the *muzungu* facilitator took him by complete surprise when she made her own confession, saying:

> I stand before you as a representative of Europeans who came to Africa, stole your wealth and turned you into slaves, who were taken into foreign lands on terrible ships to be sold as things.[2]
>
> I want also to confess the sin of exploitation during the colonial time, when you were deprived of your dignity, and your culture was belittled and considered rubbish.
>
> I also stand as a Christian in need of your forgiveness because, though missionaries came with good intentions, they still conveyed a lie – that we foreigners are superior. Finally, I want to apologize for the role of Europe in planting the seeds of division, which led to the genocide and plunged Rwanda into terrible suffering.

---

2. This was not actually true for Rwanda but was used as a generalization for colonial misuse of power.

Nyamutera was even more shocked when the Tutsi translator then stood up to make his own statement and ask forgiveness of all the Hutus in the room, saying:

> I am here in need of your forgiveness for the sin of my forefathers during the Tutsi monarchy. We mistreated your people. We took you for granted. We were masters and you were like slaves. We despised you. We insulted your dignity as human beings. I stand before you now to ask your forgiveness on behalf of my people.

Knowing the bitterness among Tutsi survivors, and their determination to speak of their pain as often as possible, the Hutu in Rwanda faced a lot of negative feelings. Nyamutera remembered with these words of confession how the other Hutu in the room were moved, many responding with tears of relief and solace. He reflected:

> No Hutu ever expected to be asked for forgiveness after the terrible genocide perpetrated by our people! People came forward to offer their forgiveness. There was a lot of hugging and crying, with others asking for forgiveness. It culminated in singing and dancing together. I left the place with my whole world challenged. Since that day I have not been the same person.

After Nyamutera completed the HWEC workshop, he was surprised once more, when Rhiannon invited him to a training session for Rwandans to carry on the healing workshops with others in their own communities. He struggled with his decision to participate in the training during a time when Rwanda was restless and relations were far from peaceful. The idea went against his better judgement at the time, as he now explains:

> To tell you the truth, I had no passion for reconciliation; my dream was to get passports for my family and leave Rwanda to go 'wherever'. I decided to attend because the first seminar had made a slight impact on me, and because of the warmth of the little *muzungu* and the uncommonly tall translator.
>
> I almost gave up the idea of going when I showed the invitation letter to my Tutsi pastor. He sarcastically asked, "What on earth will I tell the widows in the church, knowing that you are responsible for the death of their husbands?" Shame pervaded my mind as I told myself, "I am the wrong person, from the

wrong area, the wrong ethnic group, freshly back from a refugee camp which has a reputation of being the breeding ground of militia operations!"

It took me so much courage to leave my poor family at home during a time of clashes and shooting between the militia and soldiers in our area. But I could not believe the warm welcome I received when I arrived at the training; I felt I was special. Dr Rhiannon took me aside and kept on saying she wanted me to join their team and work as a facilitator. I couldn't believe my ears!

Two thoughts came to my mind – this would be a source of income for our family, but I was frightened by the idea of moving out of my region to venture into other parts of the country, where northern people such as myself were perceived as 'inherently wicked'. I couldn't blame those who thought this way because most of the militia who excelled in cruelty came from my home area.

Nyamutera's concern at being from the north not only related to events up to, and including, the genocide. At the time of this training of trainers (late-1997) the north and west of Rwanda were in the midst of chaos because of deadly night attacks from exiles coming in from Congo, followed by daily security sweeps by the Rwandan military in the war of 1997–1998. To be a northern Hutu was doubly embarrassing. Despite this Nyamutera persisted in the training. He continued

Dr Rhiannon encouraged me to pay attention and really benefit from all the teachings. I needed to deeply understand the material before I could take a workshop for others. I took this challenge seriously. Meeting people from other regions, sharing with them my shame and fears, yet being accepted by them, helped to open the way for me to serve other parts of the country.

Although I felt I had already dealt with my ethnic prejudices, I did not know if the Tutsi translator/facilitator would welcome me to the team once the European left the country. When I called my wife to tell her that I 'almost' had a job, I added, "If this tall guy allows it to happen." This showed me that healing takes time, it has to be tested by life's situations. Sometimes I thought I had overcome the problem, only to find that I was just halfway there.

The translator soon reassured me; it became clear he believed in me. Our first seminar together as co-facilitators was very hard, because it was in my home area. I was not confident, yet I was amazed by the impact of the event on the people.

Nyamutera has continued in this work since 1998, co-leading HWEC workshops throughout Rwanda, and now coordinating the work in surrounding countries of the Great Lakes region and beyond.

Standing in the Gap

The act of making an apology on behalf of a previous generation of ancestors who have caused offence to others is known as 'identificational confession', 'standing in the gap' or 'political forgiveness'. By standing in the gap, the current generation chooses to acknowledge the consequences of an unjust action in the past and to make a retrospective apology to those who have been affected. Because the greatest hurts in human history are inflicted by invasions and other forms of power abuse by people on behalf of institutions, governments and religions, it is easy for modern people to absolve themselves of any responsibility by saying, "This is not our problem, we were not there at the time, and we were not involved." Yet unless someone identifies with the offensive actions of the corporate entity, group or subculture, the wrong remains unacknowledged, the injury cannot be healed, old wounds fester and the historical hatred deepens. Saying 'sorry', even in a symbolic way, opens the door for healing and may lead to reconciliation. In the Hebrew Bible the books of Daniel, Ezra and Nehemiah each offer narrative precedents for such action, and these Jewish stories are models for applying the idea in the HWEC workshop.

Rhiannon became aware of the sense of betrayal many Rwandans felt because of the indifference of the Western world to Rwanda's distress in 1994. The 'identificational confession' segment of the workshop, which takes place on the final day, was introduced when the workshops were being tested in 1996–1997. By identifying herself as a European and apologizing for Europe's failure to actively support the people of Rwanda and not taking steps to stop the genocide in 1994, she initiated this act of confessing and apologizing for the failures of her predecessors. Then her American assistant apologized for the reluctance of the US government to take similar action.

These statements profoundly affected Rwandans, as shown in Nyamutera's narrative. That some in the Western world expressed sincere care and regret stirred many Rwandans, not only by affirming their suffering, but also to look at their own attitudes towards their fellow Rwandans. Similarly, when the HWEC included Sabamungu as translator and then as co-facilitator, and he apologized for the way his ancestors had abused their power over Hutus for many years, it moved many Hutu participants. They could not believe their ears. This paved the way for some of the Hutus to apologize to Tutsis for "What my brothers did to your families, and some of them are now trying to complete." Such apologies were previously unheard of in Rwanda.

These confessions moved participants from blaming one another to facing the truth of what members of their own group did, or desired to do, to the other group. Stating these truths brought relief and release – often expressed through tears, dancing and celebration. The changes in attitude encouraged other participants in the belief that relationships really could change in Rwanda.

Yet not all Rwandans could accept identificational confession as a viable path towards healing. In fact, during the fifteen-year genocide anniversary, Nyamutera experienced a severe public backlash when he spoke in an interview about the need for this kind of confession in Rwanda because so many women did not know where their husband's bodies had been buried. When Nyamutera suggested that Hutus could 'stand in the gap' and apologize, because he had seen the mental and spiritual benefit in so many others, some of the Hutus reacted because they too had lost loved ones and the thought of apologizing for anything was too painful for them; while among peace-builders there were those who criticized this proposal as a kind of emotional escapism. Furthermore it was no longer politically correct in some circles to refer to one's ethnicity.[3]

Obviously, not everyone can identify with perpetrators of injustice. I experienced this difficulty first-hand during a HWEC workshop in Kigali, when Rhiannon and her assistant were not in town. Because no other expatriate would be attending the workshop, one of the Rwandan team running the workshop asked me to come and repent on behalf of the failure of white people to aid Rwanda in 1994. Reluctantly, I agreed to go, even though I felt uncomfortable and told myself, "I have no reason to apologize for anything."

---

3. Nobel Peace Prize laureate, the late Wangari Maathai commented: "Today in Rwanda it is illegal to define oneself as either Hutu or Tutsi . . . the truth is that, while individuals may not make their identity public, they surely know whether they are Hutu or Tutsi." In *The Challenge for Africa* (London: Arrow Books, 2009), 216.

I fought the idea for several days, and then grudgingly attended the workshop. As soon as I arrived, I sensed deep transformation among the participants. As I sat and watched, I thought, "That is good, but I am not comfortable with my role in identificational confession. If I am to do it, how can I do it sincerely?" Like the striking of a bell, the thought came, "You can identify with white people who did nothing in 1994, not even pray. You could repent of your indifference to the events in Rwanda at the time of the genocide." For four years, I had conveniently forgotten that I had closed my eyes to the carnage in Rwanda, while enjoying the euphoria of the first free elections in South Africa and the inauguration of President Mandela in April 1994.

This unsettling 'wake-up' prepared me to accept my failure to care, which was the basis for my apology. Such confessions – both of what others did and what they did not do – are crucial to the healing of those who've experienced pain and trauma. In that moment, I became an advocate for identificational confession.

Makoriko's Healing Journey

In the following narrative, we learn of Makoriko's struggle to forgive the person who killed her first husband. Nyamutera stood beside her as the representative Hutu.

I met Makoriko in late 1997 and observed her face frozen with fear. Together with Ahimana, her diminutive and energetic second husband, they lived in Ruhengeri, the home and power centre of the late President Habyarimana. In 1997 and 1998, some residents of Ruhengeri supported the rebel aim of continuing the unfinished work of 1994. Thus militia were quietly welcomed and hidden in rural homes by day, where they were positioned to make strategic nighttime attacks. On the roadsides leading into Ruhengeri, the military cut back banana plantations and young eucalyptus to rebuff infiltration by Hutu militia into the local communities. Because foreigners needed a military escort to travel into the area, and such escorts were usually reserved for emergency UN convoys, I was unable to visit for a year, but Ahimana would visit me in Kigali. He told me, "Ruhengeri is burning, and we remain alive by the mercy and protection of God."

When I first arrived in Rwanda, Ahimana warmly welcomed me, and then proceeded to tell me that the Canadian priest who had headed up peace and reconciliation initiatives in the northwest region was one of the eight expatriates assassinated a few weeks before. Ahimana still hoped to see forces for peace in Ruhengeri and keenly discussed those possibilities during our conversations, while Makoriko sat apart from us, uncomfortable and unmoved.

Having lost many friends and relatives in the genocide and then losing his first wife to illness in early 1997, Ahimana was helped by both the PDW and HWEC. Then he arranged for the HWEC team to begin work in the Ruhengeri area, where Nyamutera and Sabamungu ran several of the workshops. Later, he asked if I would approve his new wife, Makoriko, as a participant in the next PDW, even though he knew that the priority was for staff, not spouses. He pleaded, "Brother, I am standing before you, but imagine that I am on bended knee. It is hard to do that here outside of the office, where I would be kneeling on small, sharp stones, but I am doing it in my heart! You know my wife and how she lost her first husband in the genocide; since marrying we have lived in the northwest and she lives in constant fear of being attacked. She urgently needs help."

Makoriko later corroborated this in her own words:

> At the time I was not certain of my safety. I feared the Hutu and felt I could be cut into pieces at any moment. I did not trust anyone walking down the street. I had a deep sorrow in me, which I did not know how to resolve. I carried such a huge and heavy weight inside. I had a recurrent stomach ache and constant headaches, but I didn't dare reveal what was inside of me.

After obtaining permission to attend the PDW, the process of change in Makoriko proceeded in stages. She described how someone came to Ruhengeri and spoke about how he had forgiven those who had killed his father. He talked about how he had lost his job and been discriminated against, describing this season of his life as a 'time of fire'. His statement, which moved her powerfully, was like the first stage of an awakening in her; it prepared her to attend the PDW. She said:

> By attending the PDW, I began a second stage of healing. Professor Simon taught me how to live with my loss and to feel and acknowledge the depth of my pain. I now know how understanding grief prepared me to experience the emotions that were a consequence of my loss. I saw that some of the emotions were very positive and others of them were negative. I was not to ignore the negative emotions, but to work out the

appropriate behaviour that would allow me to express those emotions without damaging other people.

In the session on forgiveness, I first needed to forgive myself for the things I didn't do and the things I could have done, but did not think to do at the time. Once I forgave myself, I was in a position to think about forgiving others. When I saw other people telling their stories, I began to open up to tell mine. The more I told, the more the pain diminished. After some days, I no longer had stomach aches or headaches.

The most important thing from my healing experience was the burden of my heart lifted from me. This was a great lesson for me – people with inner wounds need a confidential person with whom they can share their pain. By opening up I was even able to express my anger and shed tears. This gave me great relief.

When Makoriko attended a three-day HWEC in her area, she entered the third stage of her healing, where she related her faith journey to her life journey. Yet in spite of her healing progress, Makoriko was haunted by the fact that she did not know who had killed her first husband, or where he died, or where his body lay. Since no one had confessed to killing him, she did not know whom to forgive. This unresolved question gripped her with bitter feelings of resentment that stunted her healing.

At this crucial moment, Nyamutera made an identificational confession and apologized on behalf of his Hutu people. Makoriko explained the importance of that for her:

The best moment for me occurred when the facilitators understood how deeply I hurt by not knowing who killed my husband. As a Hutu, Nyamutera stood alongside of me and apologized on behalf of the unknown Hutu who killed my husband. He said, "My Hutu brothers killed your husband. As a Hutu, I am ashamed of that, and I apologize to you on their behalf . . . Now I beg you, please forgive me!"

I responded to him with the simple words, "I forgive you." This act was very powerful, for the moment I accepted his apology, I felt my deepest anguish flying away. I became a free person, and for the first time in five years, I was able to smile and look upon other people as human beings and not as ethnic categories. I went home free from fear. I was so grateful.

This experience has shaped my life. Beforehand, I condemned everyone who was related to the killers. But once I came to the place where I was able to forgive, I learned not to put everyone in the same basket and to differentiate between wrongdoers and innocent people.

Between them, Makoriko and Ahimana have eleven children – four blended from their previous marriages, three of their own (including twins) and four orphans who they adopted after 1994. Makoriko explained how her healing experiences broadened her capacity to relate to others, beginning with her own family.

The healing process taught me, if no one was around with whom I could talk, I could lock myself in my room and talk to God as if a person were present. I needed to voice what was in my mind; I did this many times and always found peace after I expressed my emotions in an appropriate way. This helped me in relating to my own children, who also needed healing. I decided to be their intimate friend, so they could open up safely, which gave us deep friendships. Now I've become an adviser to my children as they face new issues in their life.

The healing also empowered me to help many other people. I understood the pain of others and created a safe space where they could open up. I identified and grieved with them and I helped them, regardless of 'who is who'. People whose husband or whose parents were in prison came to share their pain as they faced the shame and embarrassment about the accusations against their loved ones.

At the beginning, I struggled with that. My first husband was killed in the very area where we now live, and the ones who killed him were relatives of some of the people I have supported. But this helped to affirm my forgiveness – to practice in deed what I said in words. It was a difficult thing to do, but it was possible.

I am committed to love everyone, without preference. That's not easy, and the genocide memorial month in April of each year brings back hard things to my memory, but I am able to cope well by the grace of God.

Makoriko's healing freed up her inner energy to become available first to her children and then to others. Over time, she began to help women with literacy, since lack of reading skills held many women back. As she grew in confidence, she became more open towards others. A gentle smile now bathed her face.

Sabamungu

Sabamungu grew up in exile in Uganda. His older brother died in 1979, during the liberation war in Uganda that toppled Idi Amin, and his father died in 1985. Though Sabamungu had an uncle, an aunt and many cousins still living in Rwanda, most of these relatives died during the genocide. He reflected on his upbringing and his need for healing when he returned to Rwanda in January 1995:[4]

> I was raised by a drunkard father who rarely talked, unless he was drunk. He was always quarrelsome and bitter. I was unaware of the effect this had on my life. Before I married, I lived with my two nieces and recall how bitter and quarrelsome I was with them; they were always frightened of me. Yet I thought this was the normal way of handling children. After I married and had my own children, I was a stern father who did not know how to give them affection or play with them.

When Sabamungu returned to Rwanda, he met Rhiannon Lloyd, who needed a translator for the HWEC workshop.

> When I first met Dr Lloyd, I had not yet received the help I needed to relate differently. So when I joined the healing work in Rwanda, it helped me deal with my past. I was able to pour out the pain of my childhood experiences; I started learning how to love and to give affection to my children. I am still learning!

Sabamungu also observed forgiveness as a consequence of healing in the workshop. But this did not make it easy for him to forgive:

> As a translator/facilitator in the workshop I believed in forgiveness but did not know how costly forgiveness was. I became aware during an HWEC workshop when a Hutu stood up and courageously asked forgiveness for the involvement of his family in the killings. All of a sudden, I realized we were

---

4. The material from this section is from pp. 14–15 of 'Rhiannon's Ramblings', Dec 2002.

meeting in a part of the country where, since 1959, Tutsi had been specifically targeted and killed at different times. This was also where, in 1994, my uncle and his wife were killed, and one of my nieces was thrown into a pit, along with her three children, and another niece was drowned with her six children.

In fact we saw newspaper photographs of the bodies that floated all the way to Uganda from Rwanda. It never crossed my mind that some of those bodies could be my relatives. All this raced back into my thinking at this moment, when in front of me stood this guy who was deeply moved and was just waiting for someone from the Tutsi side to reply to his confession. There was silence in the room, and no Tutsi got up to comment or react. I was normally the one to respond to a Hutu 'standing in the gap'. I sat tight and said to myself, "It is not going to be me this time."

Sabamungu with Nyamutera at memorial site   © Jon Warren / World Vision

The rest of the workshop team was wondering what had gone wrong with me. Eventually, I stood up and in tears I responded to this guy. I forgave his family and told the whole story of what lay behind my reticence to speak at that moment.

Later, as the team reflected on what happened, I realized forgiveness was very 'expensive' (i.e. costly). I asked myself, "If it was really difficult for me to forgive a person who was just standing in the gap, knowing that he was not the one who killed my people, then how much more difficult would it be for someone to forgive when they knew what had happened in their area, or walked around with a scar on their body as a result?"

Eventually, Sabamungu became instrumental in establishing the HWEC workshops in all areas of Rwanda. He became the first Rwandan leader of the HWEC, and his strong understanding of the content and process reflected how much he had come to understand through his initial role as an interpreter.

Beyond Borders

In 1998, the Government of Rwanda limited my work permit to June of that year, so that my job could be released to a Rwandan. During my final planning meeting with the HWEC team in Kigali, I surprised them by saying:

The world does not yet know that your work since 1997 is bringing about wonders in which Hutus are sharing rooms with a Tutsi for the first time in their life, and without either of them fearing they will be killed by the other.

If you continue this work and learn from the experience the way you are doing, within five years you will have such broad experience you could become world leaders in this short-term healing workshop. As you run these workshops on a regular basis, you will become aware of many of the finer points of how people heal or why they choose not to heal. At that time, I hope you will consider running an international training program for people to come from other countries to learn from you and benefit from your experience.

Today, the Rwanda HWEC team has trained regional teams to facilitate local workshops. Along with the influence of graduates from the program, this has expanded the reach of healing to many other communities within the country. Though Rhiannon remains active as a visiting mentor and team builder, the workshops in Rwanda are facilitated entirely by Rwandans, who are training new national leaders. With Rhiannon's help, some of these Rwandan teams are reaching across the border to the nearby countries of the Great Lakes Area of East Africa, where conflict and unresolved wounds remain. HWEC workshops have also been run in ten countries in Asia and Africa, and Rhiannon has adapted the work for other countries in Europe and the UK. Rhiannon and Nyamutera have drawn together the content of the workshop into a booklet.[5]

In 2012, "The School of Reconciliation – Healing Hurts, Changing Nations" was hosted in Rwanda by LeRucher ministries, Great Lakes Region. This first international training for HWEC focused on the formation of peace practitioners for the work of healing, reconciliation and community transformation. The six-week program included twenty-four participants from Africa, Europe, Australia and North America. This is a work-in-progress, which grows as opportunity, funding and energy are available. Fourteen years after meeting with the HWEC team in Kigali, in preparation for my departure from Rwanda, I was encouraged to see that people from other countries had started to come to Rwanda, not just to learn about the healing journeys there but also to train to facilitate it elsewhere.

But before I left Rwanda, even though several other agencies had began to run healing programs, I felt that it was important to explore a workshop that had been created in South Africa. In Part 4: *Hope after the Horror,* I introduce "The Healing of Memories" workshop for interfaith groups, along with three Rwandans who made substantial contributions to healing Rwanda's painful past.

---

5. This material and its Christian basis can be found by searching for "Healing the Wounds of Ethnic Conflict".

4

Hope after the Horror

"Nothing happens unless first a dream."
Carl Sandburg

Widening the Work

From the moment I arrived in Rwanda, people with needs surrounded me. Aware of my limited time and resources, the sense of pressure grew with each day. Because the healing journey is different for everyone and cannot be predicted or forced, I realized that no single program could provide all participants with a key to unlock their hearts and release them from their prisons of pain, shame, guilt and doubt.

Although the PDW and HWEC were bringing healing and transformation into the lives of individuals and communities in Rwanda, our team faced setbacks and discouragement. In parts of Rwanda, nightly incursions of militia and daily army patrols led to more deaths, with brutal acts of vengeance followed by military counter-attacks. Every morning, the names of the deceased were read over national radio, hinting at the locations where the infiltrators were active. My Rwandan friends in Kigali were afraid, disappointed, and grieving the losses of acquaintances or distant family members. They were frequently called away from work to attend clan members' funerals in dangerous areas, trips that often took a week. Moreover, HIV/AIDS was spreading as a result of the power abuse during the genocide and the breakdown of relationships after the genocide. Many Rwandans were also suffering from homelessness, poverty and malnutrition due to the shattered economy and the slow recovery of farming and seed stocks.

During this turbulent season from 1997 and 1998, I made several trips to Nyamata (south of Kigali) to meet with faith leaders and discuss their aspirations for peace. It took them time to appreciate that I did not have a grand master plan for their area, nor was I coming to drop funds into their laps. By the fourth visit, my interpreter turned to me and said, "Their conversation is so deep and complicated. I cannot possibly translate it for you. They have ideas but are still struggling with so many traumas in themselves as well as in their communities. It is really hard for them to be positive and hopeful for the future."

That day, I returned to Kigali determined to begin recruiting Rwandan staff, whom I could mentor to bring long-term healing to other Rwandans. Knowing that I would be criticized regardless of whom I hired, I asked several experienced African colleagues to join me in the process of selecting two from a list of sixteen candidates.

From the applications, written tests and interviews, we agreed to hire Nsabiyera, a Tutsi who grew up in the forests of Congo, with a degree in psychology and valuable experience elsewhere in Africa. Nsabiyera had been working with the trauma team, but now wanted to be involved in building peace.

For the second position, we chose Jean-Baptiste (*Ntakirutimana*), a well-educated, city-based Tutsi and, at that time, a Catholic. This decision meant turning down the third candidate in line, a humble school principal from the rural south, a Protestant and a Hutu. Though he was a good candidate, we needed a strong connection with Catholics in Rwanda. Moreover, if Nsabiyera and Jean-Baptiste could both work well with the general populace, it would communicate the hope of reconciliation.

Once Jean-Baptiste and Nsabiyera were oriented to the Kigali home base, I sent them to Ahimana in Ruhengeri for their field orientation and asked them to consider whether or not peace and reconciliation were possible when violence and ethnic tension were exploding in the northwest.

When they returned to Kigali, I was struck by their enthusiasm. While they acknowledged life was tough in Ruhengeri, they were encouraged to find people at the grassroots who believed forgiveness and reconciliation were possible. Their verbal report impacted me because of the hope it conveyed. Their description included thoughts like:

> On the second morning of orientation, Ahimana asked, "Did you hear the 'corn-popping' last evening? I know someone who was affected by the shooting, and we are going to a funeral."

We attended a funeral for five lads who were buried in a common grave.

Afterwards we sat in conversation with the bereaved and discussed whether forgiveness or reconciliation was really possible in Rwanda when such events continued. That exchange went for two hours and led us to conclude that among this community is a willingness to resolve issues by negotiation and forgiveness – not by force, hatred or violence.

This on-the-job training impacted Nsabiyera far more deeply than I had expected. He had found people who had not participated in any healing event but were actively thinking about the need for the healing of broken relationships. This was both rare and refreshing at that time.

Nsabiyera

While the government channelled its energy into the need for justice and churches preached incessantly on the need for forgiveness, the Rwandan society at-large seemed more focused on blame and shame. This was an indication of the pain and guilt besetting most Rwandans. But Nsabiyera played a profound role in tirelessly promoting the hope of peace and reconciliation throughout Rwanda, particularly in the difficult northwest region.

Although the concept of reconciliation seemed distant and unachievable in Rwanda, Nsabiyera spoke about it to everyone he met. When Nsabiyera was introduced to the Rwandan Minister of Justice as a member of a group working in reconciliation and peacebuilding, the Minister quipped, "I beg your pardon, reconciling whom? Reconciling what?" For months, our team of peace builders felt like a school of fish swimming against the tide while gasping for lack of oxygen, and I will return to this dilemma in Part 6.

When Nsabiyera and I began working together, we related well to each other because of our international experience and upbringing. He was a child of the forests of Congo, while the best three years of my childhood were spent living in a Javanese village with huge fruit trees, lush rice fields, pure streams, thickets of bamboo and distant, smoking volcanoes. We would sit and chat and smile about the gifts, challenges and fulfilment of growing up and surviving in a so-called 'primitive and backward' environment.

Nsabiyera spent some of the first eight years of his life in temporary shelters as his family left their home to flee from violence. In remembering those early years, he said:

> My family life was full of conflicts. My parents never knew how to settle their differences in any other way than through quarrels, insults and fighting. Life in the rural community where I grew up was built on survival of the fittest and competition. As a young lad I went through cultural initiations in which I was taught to fight and struggle in order to gain favours and appreciation from my parents and mentors. I was also taught that boys were initiated to endure hardship as a preparation for potential military service.
>
> Moreover, I was born amid the period of turmoil and wars that characterized the aftermath of independence in central Africa in the 1960s. My first eight years were spent in settlements of internally displaced people affected by civil unrest and ethnic conflicts. We lived then in total poverty and the bitterness of my parents taught me to hate our detractors and those who drove us to such destitution.
>
> Rwandans have experienced repeated violence in most of its colonial and postcolonial history, and adults passed on much of its ethnically construed bias from generation to generation. I was not spared this informal education of ethnic cleavage.
>
> Community and family conflicts and divisions negatively affected me. I held grudges and nourished a secret desire for revenge. I unreasonably rationalized, defended and even condoned acts of retaliation committed by my ethnic group towards other groups. I personally suffered the consequences as I lost energy, which was consumed by the unrest and my struggle to control my inner pain.

His family continued to suffer in eastern Zaire [now Congo] and twice lost all their physical possessions, including many cows. As he studied and matured, Nsabiyera began to live towards a hope that was not fuelled by a desire for revenge and retaliation, but rather reconciliation and peace. He explained this shift in his passions:

> I studied human behavioural sciences so as to understand the functions that underlay my personal pain and to explain the deep divisions in my community. Shortly after my studies,

despite my limited experience and the cultural prejudices gained in my youth, I endeavoured to help my church community settle differences and divisions. My efforts began to bear fruit, which greatly encouraged me, and initiated both personal growth in me and a commitment to peacebuilding processes.

When Nsabiyera heard about the deaths of thousands of people in Rwanda in 1994, he was working in Zambia. Of his courageous decision to return to Rwanda, he said, "My engagement in building peace and reconciliation efforts in the aftermath of the genocide in Rwanda was an opportunity to deepen my personal healing, commitment and learning."

Two years before we met, his father died of heart failure upon his arrival in Rwanda. Nsabiyera did not take time to grieve his loss or to visit his father's grave. "I feared funerals where people cry, and I did not like talking to people who had lost their relatives," he explained to me later. I wondered how he had managed to cope in Rwanda while working among so many people who needed to grieve their losses and misfortunes.

After completing the PDW workshop, he said, "I discovered something was missing in me. The PDW helped me so much in my bereavement." Soon after, Nsabiyera contacted his brother and asked him to accompany him to his father's grave. He recalled, "I became full of sadness, in deep sorrow, and I grieved. But I also had a profound, new experience of joy. After a long time of being distant from my dad, I now admired my father and his qualities. And the fear of talking to people who had lost relatives was gone." Because he recognized that nearly everyone in Rwanda needed help in the area of bereavement, he felt healing workshops would be the best way to bring reconciliation to Rwanda. He began to imagine ways of bringing the PDW to people at the grassroots. Yet in reflecting on his culture, he discovered the traditional practice of processing pain through communal storytelling.

Though conflict is inherent to African communities like any other society, history shows there has never before been mass destruction of human life to equal that in recent history. Whereas the pre-colonial history of central Africa was that, whenever ethnically based conflicts existed, there also existed mechanisms and cultural wisdom to help cut the cycle of violence. In order to cut off the cycle, the African wisdom and practice is to use cultural mechanisms of surfacing the pain in community groups and processing the reality by telling stories of pain caused and pain received.

Nsabiyera and I shared a common hope to use traditional African approaches to healing. In the following narrative, he describes the community peacebuilding process he favoured out of this traditional African wisdom:

> In seeking initiatives for Rwanda's conflict transformation, we have identified some approaches to help the expression of truth of personal painful memories and community hurts. These intrinsic community and cultural approaches provide mechanisms for Africans to search and find the root causes and solutions to their own conflicts, using their own understanding and means to reach their own common interest, at their own pace, progressively building on the success and learning, celebrating their progress, even on the small gains in peace. Such approaches are self-sustainable in the way they use inexhaustible human

Peacebuilding Team   © John Steward resources of skills, commitment and time, and draw on existing wisdom transmitted across the memories of generations.

These components encompass what I have called 'community transformational peacebuilding process', a community-centred process intimately drawing on the traditional wisdom of each single African community. This provides for a bottom-up course of action, which builds the potential capacity of the community to influence all the actors, from grassroots leaders through middle level leaders to the top leadership of society.

One of Nsabiyera's favourite sayings was, "The first raw material of healing is the facilitator of reconciliation and peace." He continually stressed, "Healing is foundational to forgiveness." His warm-heartedness often softened people's attitudes and gave them a willingness to discuss their situation without rancour or cynicism. He and his wife were compassionate and considerate, often sharing what they had with those who were struggling to survive.

Before my work permit expired in mid-1998, I handed over to Nsabiyera as coordinator of the peacebuilding team. He was soon invited by Nyamutera to visit Congo with the Rwandan HWEC team and co-facilitate workshops in that culture. One Congolese participant, who normally would have treated him as an enemy, adopted Nsabiyera into his family, reflecting his acceptance of difference rather than a traditional in-or-out view of clan membership.

Reflecting on his own transformation and insights from observing others' healing journeys as a workshop facilitator, Nsabiyera identified seven stages of the "complex, undulating journey of healing." Recognizing that healing journeys "are not linear, but rather highly dynamic processes involving many steps," he outlines these seven stages of his healing journey below:[1]

> First, my journey began with a desire to engage in peacebuilding work. Here I needed to look outwards and consider the needs of others. As I heard survivors tell their stories of pain, my own memories resurfaced intensely. The emotions of anger, hatred and bitterness towards the other ethnic group contradicted my commitment to peacebuilding work. I realized I did not embody the message I wanted to convey about peace and reconciliation.

---

1. A longer version of these steps was first published in Philip Clark and Zachary D. Kaufman, eds., *After Genocide: Transitional Justice, Post-conflict Reconstruction and Reconciliation in Rwanda and Beyond* (London: Hurst Publishers, 2008), 152–155.

Second, I examined my past to try to understand the meaning of my pain. What were the factors fueling my ethnic hatred? How could I understand the way to end cycles of violence? I needed a group of Hutu and Tutsi who would be willing to wrestle with such questions and to help me find meaning to what happened to me.

Third, I learned the best way to engage truthfully with others was to openly share with them and face our emotions and our wounds. I began to share my thoughts and speak of my emotions and to weep over my experiences. While I had a tendency to condemn those I felt were the source of my pain, including myself, God and perpetrators of crime, this was not enough.

Fourth, I chose to accept my past and to release myself from its grip. I needed to move from being a victim, which allowed me to claim the right to revenge and to threaten my offenders; I also wanted to be free from the pain which consumed my energy, haunted me with memories and blocked my hopes. By sharing with others and helping them I began to be liberated from my own bondage of self-pity, sorrow, anger and hatred. I found ways for my negative feelings to be transformed into virtues.

Fifth, I began to understand the benefits of freedom gained through forgiveness are primarily my own. It helped when I began to understand the causes of the hatred towards me in those who had offended me. I began to feel pity and compassion towards them. I began to understand my need to forgive others and myself. This liberated me from the hatred I had carried within.

Sixth, I could now move toward a place of reconciliation, where I believed it was possible to live and interact with people whom I previously hated. I had hated the entire Hutu ethnic group and considered them my enemies. However, as some of them shared their pain with me and expressed shame and apology on behalf of their ethnic group, I felt willing to extend my forgiveness toward them and to even apologize for the oppression of Hutu during the reign of the Tutsi monarchy in Rwanda, particularly the collaboration of Tutsi with the Belgian colonial regime. I began to build friendships with Hutus. By working with Hutus I was also involved in acts of reconciliation.

Finally, my life and my work began to flourish. I began to hear amazing stories from other people who had experienced profound healing, forgiveness and reconciliation. It gave me great pleasure to share these stories with wider audiences. Observing these changes in other people confirmed my commitment to peacebuilding and reconciliation.

Through his commitment to the grassroots, Nsabiyera encountered many powerful stories of change – including the encounter described in the next section, which he witnessed during a return visit to the Ruhengeri region in 1997.

Mama Deborah and her Dream

After his initial field orientation in Ruhengeri, Nsabiyera attended three leaders' gathering to pray for peace in the turbulent northwest region. The second meeting was interrupted by the visit of a woman whom Nsabiyera recognized as the mother of one of the five boys who had been kidnapped, murdered and buried several months before. He had attended their funeral with Jean-Baptiste, and the conversation after the burial had inspired him to believe that forgiveness and reconciliation were possible in Rwanda. The woman he recognized, Deborah Niyakabirika, held a drawing of a dream she'd had and asked the gathering for time to tell her story.[2]

Before the war, Tutsis and Hutus lived together. We didn't consider the question of ethnicity. Then, when conflict broke out, the politicians told us Tutsis caused it. We couldn't understand who the Tutsi were who did this. They just told us "The Tutsis have caused the problem, and the Hutus want revenge, so the Hutus decided to eliminate all the Tutsi." We couldn't understand that very well either.

We were so confused. I didn't know if I was a Tutsi or a Hutu because my parents had not told me about my ethnicity and they didn't know what side I should take. Then after the genocide many Hutu people went into exile, while most of the people who died were Tutsis. My brothers died also because they had

2. 'Mama Deborah,' as I later came to know her, became the subject of a film interview I did with my colleague David Fullerton in 2005. The following selections come from the transcript of the translation made by Laura Rurangwe on the day of the interview.

long noses, like the noses of Tutsis. So they took them for Tutsis. And my sister-in-law also died; she also was not a Tutsi but they thought she was.

We came back to Rwanda in 1996 and found the government had changed. The majority of the politicians were now Tutsi, but I thought that was okay. In March 1997, some soldiers came into my house. They found us praying, they sat down, and they told me they wanted my son, my seventh child. They took him outside, and I asked, "Why are you taking my child outside?" They said, "There are some questions we want to ask him."

After twenty minutes I heard shots. I went out and found they had killed him. So we buried him and mourned for him, but I kept praying, asking, "Why have Tutsis killed my son?" In exile we had been told it was safe to return to Rwanda, the place was secure. Now my child was dead by the hand of the Tutsis.

I felt hatred for Tutsis. But more than that, I thought the Hutus were my friends, but no Hutus came to help me during the burial. Only Tutsis helped. They counselled me during that funeral. So I started thinking, "Oh God, how can a person live here safely? Should I live with Tutsis, or should I live with Hutus? Which group should I trust? Which people should I confide in?

In her uncertainty and confusion Mama Deborah drew on resources which were readily available to her: she held onto her faith by daily prayer, read the gospels of Jesus the Christ and listened to the inner voice of truth. The benefit of this to her became clear, as she continued her story:

Every person I saw, I saw as a potential killer. I was really sad because I had no one to confide in. I thought I couldn't trust a Tutsi because Tutsis had killed my child, nor could I trust Hutus because Hutus had killed Tutsi. So I took time to pray. I asked God "How should I live with peace in my heart?" I prayed for five days, and then I got an answer.

At first the answer was confusing and really difficult for me. In Matthew chapter 18, Peter asks, "If a person offends me how many times should I forgive him?" When I read the word 'forgiveness', I really didn't want to hear about it. I thought I was being asked to forgive the person who killed my child, and I was not happy about it, so I stopped my prayers.

Jesus replied to Peter, "Do not only forgive seven times but seventy times seven," and I thought this was beyond my capacity. Then one day in a dream I saw a house built on a platform which stood above Rwanda, which was a place like hell at the time, and I saw these words written: "The path to heaven passes through your enemy's house." I tried to figure out a way to get there without passing through that house of my enemy – but there was no other way. Why should I pass through my enemy's house? An enemy is a person you can't share with, you can't sit and talk with them, you can't even ask for water from them. Human nature does not readily forgive.

The habit of reflective listening with a contemplative mind brought her peace in the turmoil. The dream Mama Deborah had not fully understood was repeated with additional detail that she could relate to. Her struggle to accept the message of the dream was slowly drawing her to a difficult decision, as she indicates:

I kept thinking about it and kept dreaming about that house, my enemy's house. One day I noticed in the dream picture five steps leading to my enemy's house, steps I now knew I needed to climb.

Then I heard my inner voice tell me, "There are people who are lonely, whose children and partners died, but they've managed to forgive; and you have a whole family, with only one child missing. Why do you find it so hard to forgive?"

I thought, "I have hatred in my heart and I'm not peaceful because of that." Then in a vision I saw the soldier who had killed my son, coming towards me. I felt angry, asking, "Why is this person who killed my son coming back?"

It was like a puzzle to me, but gradually I learned the lesson: In the house of my enemy is where I will begin to find real peace. To have peace one must go and sit inside in the room of our enemy's house. Then I realized this room was in the house of the soldier who killed my son.

Go to your enemy's house

The Consequences of the Dream

Deborah explained the dream to her daughter who helped her draw a picture of it. Mama Deborah gave a copy of the drawing to Nsabiyera and it is used with her permission.

1	You know God's existence?	6	The way to the cross passes through your neighbour's house
2	Praise Him	7	The hell
3	Give thanks	8	The house of my enemy
4	Pray	9	At the cross
5	Wait for God's answer	10	John 14:6

Her dream about the house of her enemy was subsequently written into a Kinyarwanda song celebrating healing in Rwanda. Written by Amiel Hagumurukundo in 1999, and titled *Healer of Our Hearts* it included the words:

Many times you suffered; you need compassion

Many times you cried for help; you need someone to help you

Help and compassion, you have blocked their way.

The way to salvation passes by the cross,

The way to salvation passes by your enemy's home,

The way to salvation passes through forgiveness.

Though Mama Deborah had never participated in any formal healing workshop or group process, she had received this moving insight through prayerful reflection on her dreams. Her narrative continued as follows:

Then I started thinking about the soldier. I really wished to reconcile with him. But I wondered, "Should I make the first move?" He was the one who offended me, why should I make the first step? It's much easier when the person who offends you comes and seeks forgiveness but when you're the victim it's really difficult to make the first response.

One day I asked my husband, "What if the soldier who killed our son comes here and seeks forgiveness, could you forgive him?" Because my husband was not there when our child died, he didn't know the soldier. He replied, "Personally I can't forgive him. If I see him I will kill him, even if they imprison me, or kill me. I would have to take my revenge." It is really difficult to forgive a person who killed your son.

Then three months after the death I saw three soldiers coming to my house and I recognized the one who killed our son in the middle of the group. I got really scared, closed the door and went and told my children, "Go and hide; the killer has come back." I said to myself, "Okay, he wants to kill me now."

The men waited, so I opened the door and asked them, "Have you come to kill me?" The soldier in the middle came and hugged me, and said, "Mama we will not kill you, and we've come to visit you." I replied, "Come in and have a seat," but I remained standing.

He said, "I have a message for you." I ran into my bedroom and started to cry. I knelt down and started praying, "Do I have to forgive him today?" When I returned to the living room, he stood up and said, "I really want to talk to you." The other two soldiers began to go outside and he gave them his gun saying, "Take my gun. She may think I am going to kill her."

I asked him, "Aren't you the one that killed my son? Do you think I've forgotten you?" He said, "It is true, I killed your son. But I've come here to seek your forgiveness." Then he told me strong words: "During the war people told me Hutus had killed my family, my parents. So I joined the military with the idea of killing all the Hutus. But now I don't want to do that. God showed me I also need parents, and I've come to ask you to forgive me and I would like you to replace my parents. Please, will you be my parent?"

I told him, "Go away while I think about that. When you come back I'll give you an answer." I really didn't mean it; I just wanted him to go.

With the tense atmosphere in Ruhengeri at that time, it was hard to imagine such a confronting interaction taking place without someone losing their life or their composure. The young soldier had something to lose, since at that time in 1997 the military were court-martialling any soldier in Ruhengeri who behaved inappropriately. It is certain that the young man knew that if Mama Deborah handed him over to his commander on the grounds that he had killed her son, he would lose his life. After a long pause, Mama Deborah continued:

Two days later I went looking for him at the military camp. I didn't know his name, but when I reached the camp he approached me and welcomed me. He hugged me warmly, but I was still wavering about him. Then he took me by the hand and introduced me to all his friends saying, "This is my Mama." How can a child, a young person, show such love to an old person like me? The other soldiers said, "If this is your mum, take her to the visitors hut and chat with her there."

Then I asked, "Do you really mean what you are saying, when you say, 'Forgive me?'" He said, "I came looking for you because God showed me I needed a parent. Since I'm still on this earth, I need a parent, like all of my friends, like all other children." He told me the war started when he was at boarding school and not living at home. I started feeling sorry for him and I realized he did need a parent.

The path to heaven passes through your enemy's house, and here I was with my enemy in his house. I thought to myself, "We need to first forgive each other and know that even if the other person offended me, I could go and offer forgiveness." We kept on talking, we hugged each other and exchanged addresses, and he told me his name. I told him the only punishment I could inflict on him was to take him in place of my son and to feed him like he was my own child.

I went home and said to my children, "My family, I'll be bringing a visitor here." Later he came to see us regularly and I'd tell my husband, "He is just a neighbour." Shortly before my husband died, I asked him, "Do you know this youth who comes here to visit us?" And he said, "The one who killed our son?" So my late husband became aware that I had forgiven the soldier. And whenever the soldier was on leave, he would come and stay at our house for a few days, and he was welcome at our place.

An uneducated woman of profound faith, Mama Deborah became a passionate advocate for forgiveness and reconciliation, taking every opportunity to tell her story and share her convictions with groups and individuals. As the sun was setting behind the mountains and the light began to dim, Mama Deborah reflected on the richness of her life and her most recent insights from the latest development:

I tell people my story. I say, "We cannot live alone, we need each other and we need one another. When we forgive, we must forgive wholeheartedly; no remorse and no regrets." Today I have nothing against that soldier. He is my child now, and whenever I meet him I embrace him. In the past when a Hutu died you would not find any Tutsis at the funeral. But nowadays it's changing. Both Tutsis and Hutus come to help and console. We have now realized that living happily with our neighbour is the best thing. Instead of considering the tribe, or ethnicity, it's better to live peacefully and in harmony.

My father, who died this year, gave us important words just before he died: "I'm giving you love as a heritage. And the love I'm giving you is 'Love with no boundary, love with no limits.'" At his funeral we were surprised by the stories Tutsis told us. There are some people who went into exile in 1959. At the funeral, they told us, "This man who is 'sleeping' here helped us during the wars in 1959. We are Tutsis, and he was a Hutu. But he didn't do what fellow Hutus were doing. He helped us escape and since that day we considered him as family."

Whenever I look at the video we took during his funeral, it really impresses me. Those Tutsis had gone to Congo, but when they came back after the war, they came and treated us as family. And at the burial they helped us; it's really something special because traditionally many Tutsis and Hutus in this area still don't like sharing or helping each other.

You know, my dad was a Hutu, but my mother was a Tutsi, so we were considered as Hutus. And previously, Hutus and Tutsis rarely shared drinks or sat down and talked together. But after the funeral of my dad, I decided we should start living together. It was high time we lived without segregation, with no discrimination, so I invited every person at the funeral and they came and shared food and drink and we all talked together. We had made one big step.

Such stories should be told all over the world. Rwanda is so lucky because people from all over the world come here to Rwanda to bring good messages that encourage people to heal and change. But we still have a problem with the youth because many parents here in Rwanda don't like Hutus marrying Tutsis.

No Hutu or Tutsi – only Rwandans!

After meeting Mama Deborah in 1997, Makoriko (whom we met in Part 3: *Taming the Trauma*) began to nurture a friendship with her. Makoriko reflected how it was, when their friendship was just beginning:

Years ago, Mama Deborah cared for my children for more than a month while I had the twins. I didn't immediately trust her, and I had some reservations about what might happen. But my fears of the Hutu melted as she dropped irresistible bombs of love, and I finally realized our friendship was profound and genuine.

As the two women began to connect as friends, Makoriko was accused by Tutsi women of being careless of her heritage and risking the life of her children, by allowing a Hutu into her house to care for them. When the two women walked down the street together, other women reacted with disapproval and disdain. And many women were shocked when the two begin to exchange and wear each other's clothes.

On one occasion, I asked Makoriko and Mama Deborah to pose for a photo together. As they groomed themselves, I joked, "People who know your stories will ask, 'Are these two very different women still good friends?' Let me prove it by taking this photograph, showing that you remain close to each other." They got close and smiled for the camera.

When I printed the photo, I was amazed to observe how Mama Deborah looked like the old colonial stereotype of a Tutsi, whereas Makoriko looked like that of a Hutu. That observation, I knew, was

Makoriko & Mama Deborah   © John Steward

false and irrelevant; but I enjoyed the moment because in their behaviour towards each other, they exemplified the eloquent statement, "Here there are no Hutu or Tutsi – only Rwandans!" When I asked Makoriko her opinion of Mama Deborah, she said, "Mama Deborah is so special that, at this moment of our interview, she is caring for my mother, who is immobile. Deborah comes to care for her morning and evening; she is a consistent person with unconditional love." Over the years, their intimate and trusting relationship has impacted many women in Ruhengeri.

In spite of the limitations of poverty and the suffering Mama Deborah has experienced in losing her husband to illness as well as her son, she is full of courage, humility, grace and gentleness. Her story has brought much hope to Rwanda; she models a life of reconciliation and devotes much time and energy to encouraging and affirming others towards a renewed and transformed mindset. The soldier she adopted continues to visit her whenever he is able to.

Jean-Baptiste

Jean-Baptiste, a trained teacher, was touched by the profound simplicity of Mama Deborah's faith. As a Christian, he too has become a model of the power of forgiveness and reconciliation.

Growing up just a few kilometres from Butare, the intellectual capital of Rwanda, Jean-Baptiste studied at a teacher training school and had a degree in philosophy. When the genocide began, he was horrified as he heard wailing, shooting and voices asking for help; then he saw dead bodies piled up in the street. On April 21 he fled to Nairobi in an emergency UN flight in an effort to protect teachers and academics by God's providence and special protection. In the following narrative, he describes his return to Rwanda after the genocide was stopped.

> I returned to Rwanda a few months after the genocide and found almost my entire family had been murdered. When I got to my hometown, it was heart breaking: all the houses were destroyed. Where there used to be about fifteen homes, nothing stood, and even the bricks were smashed to dust. I met a deaf lad who tried to explain what had happened to my kin. He was a survivor, and I thought the attackers let him live in order to tell the story, knowing he could not speak or hear anything.
>
> My conversations with the local population provided no further information of substance, apart from telling me what others did. I gathered information about the looting. Then I found the body of my mum and younger brother and buried them. Many years passed before I was able to hold a ceremony and farewell her in an appropriate way.
>
> I learned more when I went to the place where the mass killings occurred. The woman who married my brother-in-law told me they took people to the stadium and to churches where, it was claimed, they would be protected. But when they reached there, the militia and the military surrounded them. My younger brother was strong and tried to escape, but they cut him to pieces while he ran.
>
> The rest were killed at the stadium, except for my mother. She was so revered and respected that no one dared to touch her. She was allowed to return to the home village but found there the man who would kill her. He decided that, if she remained alive,

he couldn't steal her family plot, so he cruelly hacked her using traditional weapons. They thought I was already dead in Kigali, and the killing of my mother would remove the last member of the family.

As part of Jean-Baptiste's orientation to the team, I had him participate in the healing workshops, along with Nsabiyera. Jean-Baptiste was particularly moved by the final day of the HWEC workshop, when those who represented the perpetrators of injustice made confessions (identificational confession). In the following narrative, he remembers his experience during the workshop:

> I was relatively untouched throughout the workshop until the moment when Dr Lloyd identified as a European and repented on behalf of that group for ignoring Rwanda's predicament. She also mentioned the failure of the UN to act on the information it had. Then Dr Lloyd's assistant identified as an American and apologized for America's failure to act swiftly.
>
> If the West had responded quickly and firmly, it could have limited the victims of the genocide. Their confessions touched me, coming from people and nations who had abandoned Rwandans when Tutsi were being mercilessly massacred all over the country.

After the workshop, Jean-Baptiste surprised me by admitting his bitterness for the decimation of his entire family and many people in his country. Yet, before long, he played an important role in bringing a third healing model from South Africa into Rwanda.

Healing of Memories Workshop

During our time in South Africa before we entered Rwanda, Sandi had visited Father Michael Lapsley in Capetown and learned about the Healing of Memories (HOM) workshop he had developed for South Africans to work through their pain and struggles in the journey towards reconciliation.[3]

Michael had participated in the Truth and Reconciliation Commission (TRC) hearings in South Africa, hoping to discover who had sent him the letter bomb that had destroyed his hands, the sight in an eye and affected his

---

3. Michael Lapsley's biography, which is cited in the bibliography, includes a chapter on his Rwandan experiences. His website is www.healing-memories.org.

hearing. Throughout the TRC investigations, he observed that the participants were mostly leaders, decision makers and those in the higher levels of South African society. Though many people who suffered the violence of apartheid listened to the testimonies, either in person or on television, the average person had little or no opportunity to speak. In many cases, hearing details about how loved ones suffered and died added new trauma to people's lives. And seeing the decisions and actions of the apartheid government fuelled people's sense of rage and injustice. Yet there were no provisions in the TRC for onlookers to process their pain.

This disturbing reality led Michael to work with South African psychologists and other specialists to develop the Healing of Memories (HOM) workshop. In contrast to the TRC, the HOM workshop provided a safe and supportive space for every participant to share his or her story within a confidential small group. This three-day workshop invites participants to explore and respond to their feelings of loss, sorrow, anguish and pain so that they do not continue to hold those feelings in their bodies, where they foment into bitter poison.

Once the PDW and HWEC workshops were up and running, I remembered Sandi's recommendation and sent Jean-Baptiste to Cape Town to participate in the HOM and explore its potential for Rwanda. Jean-Baptiste was accompanied by Mr Kageruka, a Rwandan MP and a member of the Catholic Justice and Peace Commission, whose thinking about reconciliation and healing within Rwanda we hoped to influence.

Father Michael Lapsley   © Healing of Memories

The workshop made a powerful impact on both Jean-Baptiste and Mr Kageruka. As a white person with metal hands, Michael's visible wounds gave him good reason to be bitter and angry, yet he spoke with grace and hope. Jean-Baptiste reported that the workshop was meaningful not only because its founder had a dramatic story, it was also beautifully constructed to engage body, mind and spirit and it was suitable for interfaith groups. The process was well paced with many elements, which engaged the whole person, combining drama, artwork, music, symbol, liturgy and ritual, advocacy, prayer or poetry and celebration. Above all, it gave opportunity for each participant to tell their story with a reflective and supportive audience. Michael himself stressed that it allowed painful truth to be drawn out of a person, like pus from a wound. This HOM experience seemed suited to Rwanda because it offered one-step forward on the path to life and health after violence and loss.

In 1999, Jean-Baptiste coordinated Father Michael's first visit to Rwanda, where he met students at the Rwandan National University in Butare, Rwanda's seat of learning and the second largest city after Kigali. The students at the university responded enthusiastically to Michael's magnetic and gentle personality, as well as his hopeful and assuring words: "Every person has a story to tell, and every story needs a listener . . . I am a victim of a crime. I survived the crime. I am on a healing journey and, although I have not yet met the perpetrator to forgive him or her, I am a victor over evil, hatred and death. I am living a purposeful life."

During the visit, Michael also ran a HOM workshop along with training for future facilitators. In his book *Redeeming the Past* he speaks of his first workshop in Rwanda: "We were told beforehand that Rwandese men don't cry, but we discovered that given permission and a safe and caring space, they do cry and they did . . . I think we succeeded in providing a healing presence for those who trusted us enough to share their terrible stories."[4] Michael made subsequent visits to extend the impact of the workshops to widows and prisoners due for release. He also advised the government and other organizations involved in healing work in Rwanda and the Great Lakes Region. His work has now been brought into ten African countries. In a conversation with Michael, he told me, "I have met people in Rwanda who lost grievously and who are hurting deeply, but have managed to find a life-giving response to what happened to them; they have been able to disinfect themselves, to get rid of the poison."

---

4. Michael Lapsley, *Redeeming the Past* (Maryknoll: Orbis, 2012), 171–172.

In the HOM workshop, Michael introduced the concept of 'Bicycle Theology'.[5] Following is his account of the parable:

> There was Tom and there was John. Tom lived opposite John. One day, Tom stole John's bicycle and every day John saw Tom cycling to school on his bicycle. A year later, Tom walked up to John. He stretched out his hand. "Let us reconcile and put the past behind us."
>
> John looked at Tom's hand. "And what about the bicycle . . . ?"
>
> "No," said Tom, "I'm not talking about the bicycle. I am talking about reconciliation."

In this parable, the stolen bicycle is a metaphor for injustice, and the enigmatic way Tom sees things highlights the importance of restitution as a key dimension of justice. It also suggests how easily one can attempt to manipulate and simplify a very complex matter. Once healing has commenced, forgiveness is an appropriate response after the stolen bicycle is returned. In Michael's situation, restorative justice would involve financial or tangible physical support for the assistance he daily needs in order to live with the effects of his injuries so that he can be free to lead and train others in healing events.

In reflecting on the parable, Michael observed:

> Sometimes we reduce forgiveness to simply saying 'sorry'. But forgiveness involves returning the bicycle we have stolen. In my case, no one has acknowledged responsibility for the letter bomb that destroyed both my hands and an eye. At this stage, forgiveness is not yet 'on the table'.
>
> Perhaps when I return home today, I will find someone at my front door that says, "I am the one who sent you a letter bomb. Please, will you forgive me?"
>
> I might ask, "What do you do for a living? Do you still make letter bombs?"
>
> "No, actually, I am a paramedic because I want to be part of healing the nation." Then I would respond, "Yes, of course

---

5. This parable was first told by Father Mxolisi Mpambani in 1996, during a panel discussion on reconciliation as part of the work of the Reconciliation Commission. Michael supplied me with a copy of his own two-page explanation – see the next note.

I will forgive you. And I prefer that you spend the next fifty years working as a paramedic rather than locked up in prison. That is because I believe in restorative justice rather than retributive justice." *The difference*

After we have tea, I might say to the person I have forgiven, "As you see, I have no hands and only one eye as a result of the bomb which you sent me. Because of my injuries, I will always need to employ someone to assist me. You cannot give me back my missing limbs, but you could help me to pay my assistant for the rest of my life. That would not be retribution or revenge, but rather reparation and restitution in ways that are possible for you."[6]

Our team learned new skills through his workshop and came to a deeper appreciation for the importance of each person telling his or her own story in order to release the poisons of pain and bring the clarity that leads to transformation. When I remarked on the difference in one colleague, whose countenance had shifted from sad and sullen to vibrant and alive, she replied, "Oh yes, the HOM workshop was right for me. Someone who was so badly hurt led it; every time he spoke I saw his visible wounds, yet his face shone full of peace. His message infiltrated my thinking, that I too could be healed despite the terrible things that happened to me."

In time, the workshop became particularly useful among prisoners. One prison worker, who had trained as a workshop facilitator, remarked that the simplicity and gentle humanity of the workshop helped prisoners to open up. Some prison chaplains mediated with prison directors to have citizens from the same communities as the prisoners join the HOM process in the prison, bringing together survivors and perpetrators to work through their mutual healing. This added a restorative, inter-personal dimension to the healing journey.

Writing of his experience in the South African prisons, Michael says: "HOM workshops seek to break the chain whereby the victim becomes the perpetrator, by acknowledging the pain of the past and helping inmates to see the connection between their own mistreatment and their victimization of others."[7]

---

6. Extract from "Bicycle Theology," by Michael Lapsley, 2000, Column, *Sunday Independent*, 11th of June.

7. Lapsley, *Redeeming the Past*, 175.

Though the process of bringing Rwandan survivors into the prisons began with fear and uncertainty, it initiated a controlled and safe re-building of bridges across broken relationships. Many of the survivors pointed out to the prisoners how practical help, such as food production, house construction and repairs, assistance with education, and friendship, could return something of what was lost. And the prisoners were more open to these suggestions when they came within the safety of a facilitated small group, rather than as part of a public sentence within a formal justice pronouncement. I will further explore the work of forgiveness, apology and reparation among prisoners in Part 5: *Judging for Justice*.

Extending Generosity, not Revenge

Some years later, Jean-Baptiste made a second trip to the Republic of South Africa to attend a conference honouring the ten-year anniversary of the HOM workshop. Participants, who were mostly experienced facilitators of the workshop, came from around the world. Some former prisoners also participated in the conference. At the closing ceremony of the conference, Michael asked him to reflect on the significance of the event. And Jean-Baptiste frankly responded:

> I must say I wondered why on earth ex-prisoners were the ones asked to give the first talk at this conference. It was a considerable challenge for me to listen to the stories of ex-prisoners. I felt quite tense about this. In Rwanda, we have over 100,000 people imprisoned for their actions in the genocide.
>
> Many of us in Rwanda struggled with understanding how those who committed genocide could have caused such harm. As the ex-prisoners spoke at this event, I began to realize I was grateful I could listen to the voices of the speakers. I had never before tried to think about the perspective of those who committed the crimes in Rwanda.

When we cause someone else offense, our chief action must be to repair – to do what is right and to restore some justice. We can think of our two feet as a metaphor for justice: after we stop running away from the one we have wronged, our first foot must turn to face the person we hurt, apologize and ask for forgiveness. Then our other foot can step forward as we move towards the one we have hurt in an act of engaging and returning something of what was lost. Justice is done when restoration accompanies the apology.

But sometimes, the victim chooses to extend forgiveness to the perpetrator, even in the absence of an apology. In the next segment Jean-Baptiste describes his decision to seek out the man who murdered his mother in order to forgive him. Four years after the HOM conference in South Africa, even though the man had never offered an apology, despite prisoners being exhorted to confess, Jean-Baptiste took action, as he describes below:[8]

> I decided to meet the man who murdered my mother. I wanted to go to him and say, "You killed my mother, I forgive you, but I don't want to ever see you again for the rest of my life." It was a strategy to get him out of my life and keep him from my sight. I wanted closure, to stop dreaming about him and to keep my memory from being obsessed with him.
>
> I met and forgave him twelve years later, at God's prompting and His support and guidance. But it took me a year to prepare myself, through three rounds of fasting and prayer, each lasting forty days. During a prayer session I had a vision that I was forgiven; a vision of being forgiven from my childhood for everything wrong I had done and would do. The same voice told me, "Go and do the same." I worked on my personality and faced the difficult emotions within: of anger, guilt and shame, fear and hatred. God wanted to get my own emotions under control before I went to meet this man.
>
> So he could feel a bit secure, I chose a friend to accompany me – Nyamutera, who was of the same ethnicity as the man I was to visit.
>
> We were invited into the office of the Director of the Central Prison, and he called the killer to come and meet us. It was overwhelming. At first I was too afraid to look at him. But I stood up and greeted him, only to find he was shaking from head to toe. The director told him to tell me how he killed my mother. But I realized this was not possible in these circumstances. I requested that we continue in a private place.

---

8. While my source material was documented in 2008, some of the quotations in the following sections have since been aired on BBC radio in May 2013.

Jean-Baptiste braced himself to hear details of a story he had never fully known. His begrudging willingness to offer a superficial and speedy forgiveness was about to pay unanticipated dividends by way of information, relationship and emotional relief.

> By the time we sat he was so afraid; but he told me what happened: how the killings were planned and implemented, who was involved, where the people were killed and their bodies fell. He told me details no one had told me. He informed me he killed ten other people. At the end of the forgiveness process, he added, "Please mediate for me so I get in touch with their relatives, I want to go through a similar repentance-forgiveness process."
>
> All this took time to come out. About two hours later, he started telling me how he killed my mother. When the mass killings were completed in the stadium, she found him at the village. Then it dawned on him, "nobody else is prepared to kill her; I have to do it". He acted as if possessed by a superpower. She begged him not to kill her and covered her head, but he proceeded to hit her over the head.
>
> When he told me how he killed my mother, I was filled with grief. I partly lost my consciousness, I was crying, but through the power of God I felt my brain clear and knots were being untied inside me. I felt lighter within, as if I had lost half of my body weight.
>
> From that moment on I was completely relieved of grief and hard emotions. I told him I had not come to see him of my own will. God had placed his grace on me and I had come to do the same to him, by God's request. I did it in full awareness of my actions.

The questions Jean-Baptiste asked after he had heard the truth reflect the generosity, which – true to his mother's name, Generoza – he offered to the man who so shamelessly killed her. He chose to offer good for evil, generosity instead of revenge. Jean-Baptiste continued:

> I could not see any sign of remorse during his confession. I was amazed by his insensitivity and his inability to appreciate my feelings and my efforts in coming. I asked, "if he had the chance, and I could bring my mother back, what would he tell her?"

He said, "I would ask for money because she used to give me money." I said to him, "Good I'll give you the money you want, tell me how much you need. Is there anything else you would ask?"

"I would ask for a prison uniform, mine are shabby."

I said to him, "I will give you two sets of uniforms. Tell me something else that you would ask my mother."

Then he said, "I would ask her to come and visit me in prison." "I will be coming to visit you in prison," I replied. I was surprised by his reactions.

Then Nyamutera, who was supporting me, remonstrated with him, "Can't you even ask for forgiveness?" And then he asked my forgiveness. Before coming to see him, I had met with my three nieces for four hours and asked them if I could forgive this gentleman on their behalf for his killing of their grandmother. They allowed me to do this. I told him this forgiveness was from me and my nieces, who were the only surviving members of my family. He cried, but I could see in him a sense of relief. He told me he didn't expect me to forgive him. He said he expected I would want to kill him. Then he started tapping his hand on my leg, and he began to become a completely transformed person.

After three hours I left the prison; I felt like a new human being, full of happiness such as I had never experienced. It was a liberation, which I never thought I could ever have. My desire was that he would be released so that together we could empower others who were held back by anger, hate, fear and guilt.

I was in awe of Jean-Baptiste's capacity to love and forgive so generously, covering over a multitude of sins. I was encouraged by his hopes and his work in support of other people, seeking lasting peace within themselves and their countries.

His story also filled me with anticipation for the 'message' of change to continue its slow spread around the communities, over the hills and beyond. While I was no longer present to the day-to-day expansion and impact of the ongoing healing work, by only visiting periodically my absence freed Rwandans to decide, act and manage. They were taking the lead, learning by their own experience, within their own customs and ways of life.

My Reflection

The contribution and commitment of those we have met so far in this book gave me hope that the horror of the genocide and its difficult consequences were slowly being moderated by healing and progress. Rwanda was coming alive on many levels. In 1998 I began to draft a reflection of my first months in Rwanda. But it was an unfinished poem. With time I added that which I saw emerging and over-shadowing the sadness and troubles of 1994-98.

The poem ponders two challenges: Firstly the struggles of the fledgling new nation re-forming and coming alive out of the maelstrom and complexity of genocide. Secondly the jaundiced view of many people elsewhere, which I met as they glanced from a distance towards the country of Rwanda through darkened lenses of their mind and their expectatons, that things must always be bad in a place like that. Yet I saw emerging the potential to overshadow the sadness and troubles. I indicate something of the progress towards generosity through profound change and fresh hope, which was emerging from those who were healing their grief, offering forgiveness and restoring relationships.

I WONDER AS I WANDER
(the country of Rwanda)

No food for sale – but poison is available
See what that can cause when you put it on the table
Such nice people – with really tough lives
A silent church – expecting others to repent
But quiet about its own past

Humans not crazy – just going mad
Not enough houses for people to stay
Yet many destroyed homes.
Would I live in the same street
as the murderer of my children?

Prisoners by the prison-full – sick to death of waiting
Afraid to talk about what happened.
No-one responding to the Genocide Law,
in case they become a further statistic

If you're going for a wander said our friend
Then I wonder what you'll really get to see.

No, we're going to Rwanda, said I to the friend
That's as specific as I can be

His smile dissolved, his face was tight,
Are you O'K, will you be allright?
If you wander in Rwanda, then I really wonder...
His voice dropped off in fright

Forget the rhyme, it's too neat for Rwanda
We need something ragged and jagged and jarring
Something that tears at your heart
And pulls complacency apart
That leaves your emotions gasping
And your heart a-gaping
That gets under your skin
I've let the real Rwanda in, and I find there:

People of grace and hope and resilience
Of tears and sorrow, of loss and persistence
And people of healing, grace and apology
Forgiveness and tolerance,
An impossibly hope-filled story!

In the next Part, *Judging for Justice,* I trace the dramatic and unique role that traditional Rwanda's own culture played in bringing restorative justice to over 130,000 prisoners and several million traumatized Rwandans. In these unprecedented Gacaca trials, the world stood by and watched with astonishment and wonder at the gems Rwandans gathered from among the ashes of the genocide.

5

Judging for Justice

"If the truth hurts, just think what a lie can do."
Monique Lisbon

An Urgent Cry for Justice

Early in 1998, a Rwandan official told me about a young girl who had found the bones of her mother and taken them for burial. As the ceremony commenced, she was composed, but when the priest spoke, the girl began to shake. They stopped the ceremony and asked her if anything was wrong. She said, "Nothing is wrong," so they continued. As they were about to place the coffin in the grave, the girl groaned, rushed towards a man and began to beat him on the head, shouting, "You killed my mother." Some in the crowd grabbed the man, beat him and threw him into the grave, threatening to bury him alive.

A local official ran for help and brought the army, who subdued the group, got the man out of the grave and arrested him. They told the crowd that if anyone present had any charges against another person, they should complain on the spot and let the government deal with the issue. This event shook people out of their complacency and freed them to make on-the-spot accusations against others, resulting in nine arrests. Such stories highlighted the dangers of civilians resorting to 'the law of the jungle' to get justice – or take revenge. Through events like this, it became obvious that while many were already in prison and awaiting trial, others went free because people were too restrained to accuse another.

As early as 1995, those who had been accused and arrested for their involvement in the genocide were offered reduced sentences if they made detailed confessions and named their accomplices. Yet many of the killers who had not been arrested and imprisoned threatened to do away with confessors or witnesses and their families. These lawless death sentences were undermining the government's attempts to uphold the rule of law. Thus a national conversation began about how to enact justice for the perpetrators of the genocide.

By 1998, Rwanda's jails held 130,000 prisoners – mostly men. Over 95 percent of these prisoners had been implicated in the genocide. Many of the prisoners had been identified when people returned to their home areas in 1997 to register for new identity cards, which no longer included an indication of ethnicity. Obtaining an identity card was expensive and time-consuming for those who had lived outside of the country for many years. Yet anyone who did not have a new card could be arrested for trying to avoid recognition in the community.

In April 1998, the leadership of Rwanda staged public executions of a few who had been tried and found guilty of planning the genocide. Twenty-one men and one woman were taken to five stadiums around the country and shot. Local businesses were closed and people were exhorted to witness the punishments. The evening news announced, "Now we are beginning to see justice in Rwanda." Yet this punitive justice did not bring healing to the country, but rather further traumatized and divided people.

Community Justice

In the wake of these executions, conversations began about how the Rwandan government might revive *gacaca*, a traditional Rwandan process of conflict resolution. Gacaca is a Kinyarwanda word, which means 'grass'. When there was conflict within the community, the elders would gather the two parties on the grass and seek to resolve matters with the goal of the restoring the relationship between the two sides. By remoulding the traditional gacaca, the Rwandan government developed a community justice process in which thousands of survivor-victims came face-to-face with those who had destroyed their homes or killed, disabled, abused or harmed their loved ones. The perpetrators heard of the pain they brought to the survivors and were given the chance to tell their side of the story. The hope was that offenders would confess, ask for forgiveness, and agree to compensate or restore something of what had been lost or damaged by their criminal behaviour. This would help genocide survivors know how their loved ones had been killed and also give them opportunity to extend forgiveness to those who had harmed them and their loved ones.

Munyeli

In Part 2: *Looking for Light,* we met Munyeli, a widow who lost her parents and siblings in the genocide. In 2000, she left her role as administrator of the PDW and became the community educator for launching and mobilizing the Gacaca tribunals across Rwanda. She and a team took time to prepare and then went out to the community, sensitizing people to the content of the law and the benefits it offered for survivors, criminals, and the whole community. As someone who had suffered and survived the genocide and journeyed through her personal healing, Munyeli had been able to forgive in her heart the family's killers, and she also believed in restorative rather than punitive justice. She reflected on the roots of the traditional gacaca justice process:

> Gacaca was inspired by the Rwandan traditional justice of long ago. Whenever somebody would commit something bad they were brought to the community and asked to explain what they did and why they did it. The community would decide how to deal with that. Normally it was for minor crimes like stealing or insulting another. But when blood was involved, it wasn't dealt with by traditional gacaca.
>
> When blood was involved, blood had to be shed by a member of the accused family. So revenge was the only option. If you killed somebody in my family, then I had to kill somebody in your family. People paid careful attention to how they related to one to another, because there was no alternative for bloodshed. Blood equalled blood.

Historically, revenge and resentment were the only ways people had for responding to bloodshed. Some Rwandans had resorted to this, which if unchecked, could have destroyed even more people than the genocide. The country needed a different way to heal, but many feared the word 'reconciliation', as it implied an amnesty for those who had committed genocide and ignored the pain of the genocide survivors. Some thought reconciliation meant saying 'sorry' – which was a difficult word to hear from the mouth of any perpetrator. Munyeli observed that the government of Rwanda faced a seemingly insurmountable challenge. An excellent communicator, she nevertheless recalled how difficult it was to prepare genocide survivors for gacaca:

> I was talking to a group of genocide widows, and asked them how they would react if someone came to confess, "I killed your husband, your children, your neighbours and your relatives. Now I'm coming to ask you to forgive me because I feel bad for what I did."
>
> The group expressed feelings of anger and some even asked, "How can I forgive them when they did not even spare my baby?" Not all of the widows were able to accept the need to forgive. Unless one undertakes the journey of healing, forgiveness is difficult to understand. This is because it is not an intellectual activity, but it is something that engages the whole person, deep inside.

Many Rwandans were concerned about how justice would be enacted with so many criminals. Moreover, some innocent people had been imprisoned, while many criminals remained free in the village, without consequence. Other people feared that wealthy perpetrators would bring experienced lawyers to defend themselves, resulting in the liberation of those who were not innocent, while many who were not guilty might be punished simply because they didn't have the resources to hire a lawyer.

As Munyeli recalled, "The genocide was too enormous to be dealt with using traditional gacaca, but the government was inspired to create a renovated gacaca and involve all Rwandans in the process. The killings happened in the community. The people watched it. They saw it. They knew who did it. They knew who didn't do it."

Yet, in the end, professional lawyers were banned from any involvement in the gacaca proceedings. Not surprisingly, many international legal scholars and human rights advocates dismissed gacaca as a form of mob justice. A few western experts said it couldn't possibly be just or effective in Rwanda. Despite fierce debates lasting several years, the government of Rwanda adapted the revised Gacaca Law, and proceeded to implement it with the financial support of many donors including the UN.

The Gacaca Law established four categories of prisoners. Category I prisoners were the planners and those who had committed sexual assault and rape, and they were tried through the normal legal system. (Later, they were also included in the gacaca process.) Categories II, III and IV were tried through the gacaca community justice process when it was launched.

Category II prisoners were those accused of killing, or their accomplices. Those who were found guilty received a sentence of ten to fifteen years in prison. A voluntary confession reduced the sentence to between six and seven years, with half of the time devoted to community work. Youth who were between the ages of fourteen and eighteen in 1994 were dealt with more leniently. Those who were younger than fourteen were given amnesty and released.

Category III prisoners were those who had assaulted people without the intention to kill. The normal prison sentence was five to seven years. A voluntary confession reduced the sentence to between one and three years.

Category IV prisoners were those who looted or destroyed possessions. The normal sentence was a settlement, where the offender paid back what had been taken or destroyed. If a voluntary confession was made, they could negotiate by private arrangement with those whose possessions had been looted. The focus of all sentencing in this category was on community service and compensation.

Promoting Gacaca

For genocide survivors, the benefits of the gacaca tribunals included knowing what happened to their loved ones and who killed them, as many of them were hiding or absent during the killings. Survivors were given the opportunity to observe the attitudes of the perpetrators and identify those who were humble and repentant.

For genocide perpetrators, the benefits of the tribunals were liberation from guilt and restoration to the wider Rwandan family through contrition and confessions, apologies, reduced prison sentences and opportunities to make amends. Many perpetrators were afraid to share what they had done in public, so the Gacaca Law permitted written confessions of who they killed, how they killed, who was with them, which houses they destroyed, and what properties they looted. Writing confessions prepared prisoners to tell their stories in public and helped them analyse their behaviours and understand the seriousness of their crimes.

The gacaca tribunals also benefited the general population, as innocent Hutus did not have to carry the shame about what other Hutus did. Moreover, genocide survivors were freed from the burden of fear and suspicion of all

Hutus. Munyeli reflected on how the revised gacaca tribunals were to bring deeper healing to Rwanda:

> By addressing these complex issues, gacaca would minimize the risk of genocide re-occuring in Rwanda. Rwanda's experience in the genocide was unique and resulted in many Rwandans saying "no" to revenge, but also "no" to the law of impunity. If anyone were to bring back the politics of division and hatred in this country, they would face a mighty challenge, because we can see the benefits and urgency of stopping the cycle of violence.

To run the local tribunals, each community council elected nine tribunal judges, the *inyangamugayo* (literally translated as "person of integrity"). These judges, dominated by the Hutu majority, had to have good reputations in the community and must not have participated in the genocide. In the end, over one-third of the judges who served on the more than 11,000 local tribunals throughout Rwanda were women, who were traditionally excluded from leadership platforms within the community.

To connect and create understanding within local communities, the gacaca mobilization team, which was led by Munyeli, placed billboards about gacaca on roadsides, initiated a nationwide educational radio program and showed the film *Ukuri Kurakiza* (Truth Heals) in every district and in the prisons. They also trained more than 300 mobilizers to conduct training about gacaca in every province of Rwanda. Finally, they provided extensive training for the *inyangamugayo* judges on collecting evidence and comparing it with the testimonies of the accused as well as survivors in order to make reasoned assessments.

Educating Prisoners

Munyeli also visited prisons to prepare the perpetrators for the gacaca community justice hearings. Some prisoners had already confessed without any expectation of being released, asking for forgiveness by writing letters of apology to the survivors. Munyeli noted the impact of truth telling on these prisoners: "While they were resigned to the probability of spending their remaining days in jail, in their spirits they were free."

With time, other prisoners started to confess because confession enabled plea bargaining. If the community forgave a prisoner, his prison time could be halved. The confessions were analysed by lawyers before being accepted, and the law was clear that if a false statement, or partial confession, was discovered, the confessing prisoner could not have their penalties reduced.

Those who were approved for provisional release had to have their stories validated, corrected or expanded by the general population during the public trials. The confessions of prisoners and community responses also helped identify those who had participated in the genocide, but were still enjoying their freedom. Once identified, they would be arrested and brought to justice in the gacaca courts, but without the leniency offered to those who had told the truth.

The prison education process created awareness among inmates that a day of reckoning was coming. Prison authorities actively promoted the value of telling the truth, as did church and civic groups. The impact of truth-telling on those prisoners who confessed inspired and prepared many other prisoners to make confessions.

Bembereza

On a sunny afternoon in west Rwanda, I met with Bembereza, a prisoner in the Gisenyi prison. We sat in a tiny room with thick cement walls, which felt like a dungeon. No guards were present, but Ngabo, a pastor who worked in the prisons and served as our translator, accompanied us. Bembereza explained how he had grown in his faith during his time in prison:

> I had a burning desire to be closer to God. One night I dreamed I was fishing in Lake Kivu, which divides Rwanda from Congo, and a dove landed on me. I knew this was a symbol of peace and acceptance. No witnesses saw me kill during the genocide, but I knew I could not be baptized as long as I was hiding the truth about my involvement. In my heart I decided approval from God was more important to me than the approval of an earthly tribunal.

Sweating profusely, Bembereza told how pastors, visitors and officials had come to the prison to hear the confessions of prisoners, but at that time he only admitted to some trivialities. On the Sunday following the confessions, a group of fellow-prisoners were to be baptized. The courtyard was crowded with several thousand inmates in their pale pink tops and shorts, while around them were hundreds of guests and visitors and a choir. Bembereza felt a burning within, and his conscience told him to repent and tell the truth. As other prisoners took the microphone to make their admissions, he struggled to find the courage to speak up. At the last moment, he moved to the microphone, looked at his audience, and said:

> I am in prison for a minor infringement. Nobody is aware that I am a person who participated in the genocide. I killed a pastor, a good man – one who helped me and often gave me a lift in his car. I killed pastor Bosco in an isolated place, and nobody knows the location, except me. Today, in front of you all, I want to confess my action. To the whole of Rwanda, because these proceedings are being recorded for television, I ask you all for forgiveness.

Bembereza went on to explain to me how, as he talked, he saw the daughter of his victim in the visiting choir, so he faced in her direction and said, "I want to apologize to the daughter of the man I killed. Whether or not she can actually forgive me, I am truly sorry and offer her my apology."

With tears streaming down her face, the young lady, Delphina, ran towards Bembereza and embraced him. Between sobs she said, "I have been praying that I might know the person who killed my father, and find out how it happened and where his body lies." Knowing these details was helpful in the grieving process, as they usually provided an opportunity to locate the body and give it a proper burial.

Bembereza continued: "After a moment of burning in my heart, joy came. I felt I could just fly. Then I had an inner quiet within." Unbuttoning his shirt collar, he told me that since his confession, he had felt at peace, even though many of the other prisoners had become angry at him and called him a fool. Some of them taunted him, "Now they are going to kill you or a member of your family (in revenge)." Other prisoners harassed him about whether he would tell the authorities who they had killed. "But I have said nothing about them," he said.

Tears came to his eyes. "My family rejected me because of my confession; they've stopped coming to visit me. Everyone asked why I told the truth, because I was so close to my release date, and I could have gone free." My translator interrupted to explain that visitors brought supplementary food; the diet in prison was not sufficient for a person to live on. Bembereza was suffering since his relatives had stopped their visits.

The late afternoon sun streamed through the bars of the one tiny window, its light reminding me of Bembereza's choice to bring the truth of his deeds into the light. He continued, "Since that time, I have seen Delphina again.

I made my peace with her and her family." Bembereza sighed, as if he was looking at his situation with some wistful regret. He paused, seeming to be lost in reflection, and then continued:

> I don't know why I killed. Perhaps it was the satisfaction of evil, which made it feel like I was doing something good. Of course I expected I would not be punished for it. I had been drunk the night before – the militias in '94 were often drunk, always pressing Hutu men to "Prove you are a true Hutu by killing a Tutsi." The *interahamwe* were trained to kill, I was not. It was an impulse for me when I killed this man on 8 April 1994. I fled into Congo in July and lived in one of the refugee camps until 17 November 1996. I returned to Rwanda and remained free until 28 April 1997, when I was arrested over a minor problem concerning a vehicle.

An intoxicated, armed guard abruptly came to the window and gruffly ordered Bembereza to return to his cell. Bembereza said, "I hope what has begun in me for good will remain." I said my brief thanks and the guard led him away.

Although I did not meet Bembereza again, I learned from Delphina that when she went to the prison to meet him for the second time, he said to her: "I have made you an orphan, and you have suffered loss because of what I did. I want to give you my vehicle as a small compensation for the terrible loss I have brought upon you. My property was confiscated when I was arrested, but I have written letters for the court to release my car to you."

Despite Bembereza giving Delphina information about the place where he murdered her father, she was not able to find his remains. Delphina said she did not intend to bring any complaint against Bembereza, thus resolving his case without his participation in gacaca.

Delphina reflected on how amazing it was to be in Gisenyi on the day of Bembereza's confession. The day before, she had been in Kigali, and a friend had rung to tell her the choir would be singing in the prison. Although it had not been in Delphina's plan to be there, she had felt prompted to make the long bus ride back for the occasion.

Mama Deborah, who we met in Part 4: *Hope after the Horror*, was a victim who forgave and then adopted her son's killer after having a vivid dream. Bembereza, a perpetrator, was also moved by a dream to take responsibility for his actions and make his confession. This personal decision impacted his inmates, as it helped them face their own realities and to prepare for their involvement in the gacaca tribunals.

The Gacaca Process

Though I had returned to Australia before the first gacaca community courts opened in 2001, I made regular visits to Rwanda. Between 1999 and 2008 I entered Rwanda every 6 months to monitor progress and mentor healers and peacebuilders. On those return visits, my Rwandan colleagues frequently lamented the intensity of regularly attending the weekly gathering of their local gacaca tribunals: "Why are these prisoners telling everything in such detail? Do we really need to know how this person was killed and that person was dragged around, this group was mistreated, and that house was destroyed? It is all too much for our ears!" Through these detailed confessions, the prisoners were speaking the truth they had long been holding inside themselves. But the confessions were only the beginning, as witnesses from the community were given opportunity to validate, correct, expand or contradict the testimonies.

The Gacaca Law required a quorum of at least one hundred members of the community to witness the confessions. Each community member present was free to tell what they remembered. Some who had shifted elsewhere came back to their home area to give their input. Then the *inyangamugayo* judges had to research and cross-check the testimonies with other statements and applicable evidence. There was a lot of corroboration of evidence leading to a recommendation from the judges to the district level. Finally, a court of appeal was available. By the end of the gacaca tribunals, around a quarter of all cases were put to appeal. All this took time.

Observing Gacaca

I was fortunate to attend both an urban and rural gacaca tribunal. The rural tribunal was held in the open air outside a community centre, nestled within a spectacular vista of green hills and terraced mountains. A large contingent of women in colourful clothes sat on the grass under umbrellas waiting to witness the proceedings. The men, dressed in sober black and brown clothes, gathered in groups and stood to one side. The *inyangamugayo*, wearing identifying sash, looked significantly younger than many of those present. With gravity and purpose, they directed proceedings, taking time to consult each other in between reporting their findings, asking questions of the defendants and clarifying matters with the survivors.

When the defendants were called, about a dozen men stepped forward, shuffling nervously, looking down at the ground or towards the tribunal, rather than at the well-dressed family members of the survivors seated opposite. One woman stood and made a passionate plea on behalf of the defendants for leniency, as the plaintiffs pleaded for compensation of their physical and property losses. I could sense the challenge for the judges to realistically assess the possibility of satisfying the hopes of the victims in the context of rural poverty.

We were not able to stay to the end of the day's painstakingly slow proceedings, but I was struck by the patience and decorum of the many women from the community who observed the proceedings. They had been attending these deliberations for weeks, either as a widow or survivor waiting for a case to be heard in their favor, or as a spouse about to hear their husband receive a ruling that would impact their households, lifestyles and future relationships.

The urban gacaca was held in a hall and involved an appeal hearing on a previous decision. Though the debate between the two participants was heated and confrontational, the *inyangamugayo* diffused the intensity with a clear and firm ruling. After the session was concluded, the *inyangamugayo* explained to me their thorough work in preparation, research and review for each case. After reaching a decision, they proposed an appropriate action and/ or penalty, which went to the district level for ratification. Though the work was very difficult, the trials were bringing some justice to the survivors while the perpetrators who cooperated increased their potential to be returned and restored into their community.

I was impressed with the confidence shown by the tribunal members. Clearly they had learned by doing. But the hard work was palpable – it felt like tiny mills of justice slowly grinding out grains of truth and hope to nourish the people and country of Rwanda.

Gacaca Achievements and Challenges[1]

Between 2001 and 2010, over 400,000 suspects were tried through the gacaca tribunals. Of these, 4,000 were sentenced to life imprisonment; 40,000 continue to serve their full prison sentence for being untruthful or incomplete in their testimony; the remainder have been returned to society. Over its nine-year span, the total financial cost of the gacaca courts was fifty-five million dollars, much cheaper than any known alternative for bringing justice to Rwanda.[2]

By involving the mass participation of citizens, the Gacaca Law of 2001 provided a grassroots justice process the likes of which has never been seen in the history of the world. Drawing together both victims and perpetrators of the genocide in open, emotional hearings, the gacaca tribunals took a psychological toll on everybody, reflecting the shifting moods and experiences of each community. The focus of the hearings was: truth, peace,

Gacca group process   © Dave Fullerton

---

1. Parts of this section reflect a presentation made by my nephew, Dr Philip Clark, at Melbourne University on 28 September 2010. I quote with his permission. The talk, given one week after the Rwandan gacaca process officially ended, was an introduction from his book *The Gacaca Courts, Post-Genocide Justice and Reconciliation in Rwanda* (Cambridge: Cambridge University Press, 2010).

2. This was equivalent to one fortieth (or 2.5 percent) of the $2.2 billion used by the International Tribunal for Rwanda, which met in Arusha, Tanzania and handled less than 100 cases in fifteen years!

healing, forgiveness and reconciliation, along with Catholic themes such as atonement, penance and mercy. It provided a comprehensive form of justice at all levels of society. Hearings were conducted in everyday language, without the forensic and legal terminology of formal court proceedings, which nurtured a spirit of solidarity among genocide survivors.

However, because the quality of evidence varied enormously, many individuals were able to use the system for their own benefit. Moreover, gacaca only dealt with genocide crimes – not revenge killings. Furthermore, because the process aimed at reintegration and accountability, some survivors felt the sentences were too lenient. Some were also critical because the community service requirements imposed by the tribunals were not always met, and compensation for losses incurred during the genocide – while awarded in theory – were rarely paid in practise.[3]

The *inyangamugayo* – the wise, elected leaders who voluntarily witnessed the gacaca proceedings in each community – had to gather and clarify a lot of background information to determine the truthfulness of statements. Their responsibility carried emotional weariness, and they were often 'paid back' in the form of backlash, challenge and criticism.

As the truth was told, the gacaca tribunals often reignited memories and brought a heightened sense of threat and fear of further attack for survivors. This extended the agony of victims and often traumatized the relatives of the perpetrators, who were hearing, for the first time, details about what their loved ones had done. Many women were disgusted by the way their spouses behaved in 1994, and so they chose to live as widows rather than carry daily embarrassment for their spouse's actions.

Because people often expressed strong feelings of anger that had been held inside for a long time, the gacaca proceedings also raised tensions that required further mediation and healing. Perpetrators who were released and returned to their home villages sometimes found themselves working side-by-side with the mother of the children they had killed or the daughter of a father they had killed. For these perpetrators, there was no easy way to prove to survivors that their regrets represented a transformation of their values and beliefs in daily life.

---

3. Though nothing could be done to fully compensate for what happened, the government established a fund to improve the living conditions of survivors by helping to pay for medical care, education and housing.

The best gacaca outcomes occurred when the perpetrator visited the family of their victims to apologize and offer penitence in the relative privacy of the home.

Responding to the Limitations of Restorative Justice

One of the mottos of the gacaca process was: "Telling the truth is a healing in itself." Though speaking the truth helped the perpetrators, who had locked away their guilt for years, simply telling the truth did not bring about healing for them or for the survivors.[4] As Munyeli observed, "Many Rwandans have not had an opportunity for healing. What is being done in the healing work is like a drop in the ocean. It's tiny compared to the numbers of people who need healing." Munyeli also reflected on the problem of making restitution in the context of the widespread poverty of post-genocide Rwanda:

> All those killers, the *interhamwe* (militia) who took machetes, they have nothing to give back. So if our justice is based on our capacity to make recompense, then only the top leaders can be forgiven – those who have houses and land, which they could sell . . .
>
> One prisoner who confessed said, "You kill me and resurrect me, and kill me again and again . . . Until you have killed me more than ten times. That would cover what I have done. Otherwise, there is nothing I can do compared to what I did to those people."
>
> When somebody says, "I am sorry" don't you think that is a form of compensation? You've killed my relatives and you come and say, "I am sorry." Yes, you are sorry – you do have to do something, but you do what you can, not what you cannot do. You can't bring them back – so you do what you can. Such prisoners have to help rebuild the country; they have to work, to do something. They are put to work building roads, hospitals, clinics and houses for survivors as requested by the local communities.

In response to the challenges posed by the proceedings, the Episcopal Commission for Justice and Peace (ECJP) trained more than 1,000 monitors to help communities through the gacaca process. These monitors improved the gacaca hearings by advising the leadership about the concerns of those

---

4. Healing involves making some sense of memory's pain, says Roslyn White, and gacaca by its nature could not do that for every participant.

who didn't feel comfortable voicing them. They also bargained with proposed settlements when perpetrators families were unable to afford the cost of their penalties. Most significantly, these monitors united people after the process and visited individuals to offer them counselling and support when they were observably re-traumatized.

Thus the gacaca helped set the atmosphere for ongoing conversations that changed perspectives and led to transformed attitudes and outlooks, which eventually enabled stories of forgiveness and hope to emerge.

Beyond Gacaca

One stormy day, colleagues from my team gathered in Nyamata to meet with members of The *Ukuri Kuganze* Association (UKA), which means, 'Let truth prevail', or 'Truth will triumph'. As we walked into the tiny office, twenty people were quietly singing in gentle, peaceful harmony. This disparate group of Rwandans was made up of ex-prisoners, widows, survivors, returnees and relatives of existing prisoners and were committed to promoting truth-telling, healing, forgiveness, and reconciliation in their communities by telling the story of their healed relationships. Yet because they knew that forgiveness was difficult when so many people were struggling to meet the basic needs of life, they were also committed to working together to restore communities by building houses for widows and the homeless and raising goats for economic assistance.

Buhanda, the UKA secretary, admitted that not everyone in the community was supportive of the association because the group included ex-prisoners. But because the group members had built more than 150 straw-mud houses for survivors and had distributed two hundred goats to needy widows and survivors over the previous ten years, many resistant family members had begun to listen to Buhanda's message: "Unless we reconcile, we will lose our life in another war." He explained how members had taken this message of reconciliation and forgiveness to schools, local government, public meetings. "I think the *Ukuri Kuganze* Association deserves the Nobel Peace prize for promoting reconciliation," he told me.

Musabyimana and Buhanda

Musabyimana, another member of the UKA, confessed to killing three people with his own hands and promoting the death of many others as he pointed out targets to other militia. He participated in the killings because he hated Tutsis and believed they were bad people: "My grandmother always told me Tutsis were bad and had killed many people. I developed a severe hatred of them. Whenever I was grazing the goats with my peers, I would harass the Tutsi goatherds. Even as I read my Bible I kept showing my hatred of them."

Musabyimana explained that, after the genocide, he tried to escape from the area with his family, but when they reached Lake Kivu in the west, they couldn't get a boat to take them across, so they were forced to come back home. "Then my conscience began to trouble me," he said. He became sick and began to hate his own family. "I went and lay on my bed and heard a voice speak clearly to me: 'Why did they die? Why did you kill them?' I realized the skin of my victims was the same colour as mine, and I wept." In his confusion, he cried out, "God forgive me," and a peace came into his heart because he felt like he had received mercy. Then he heard a voice that said, "Be calm, and do not worry. You will not be killed, but you will be jailed." Musabyimana continued:

> My heart went from burning hot to peaceful, as if a gentle wind were blowing through me. Even though my friends had chosen to not speak the truth, even if they were tortured, I decided I would tell everyone what I had done – even though people in the community pressured me to remain silent. The next day I was arrested and taken away to the Kigali prison. It was October 1994, six months after I had participated in the killings.

In prison, torture was the normal way to obtain confessions. When soldiers came and began to beat him, he protested, "I will answer all your questions because I know my truth. I have nothing to hide." The prison prosecutor doubted this and called him to listen to the testimony of two witnesses and a reporter, whom they had brought to accuse him. "These people will tell the truth about what you did," the prosecutor said. Musabyimana agreed with everything they reported and added, "What these witnesses said is true, but they did not tell you the whole story. There were other things which they did not see." The prosecutor was shocked and asked if he had been tortured or if he was mad, because he could not believe that Musabyimana was choosing to tell the truth. Eventually, Musabyimana signed six pages of notes with his admissions. Then his fellow prisoners began to fear he would tell the truth about them, so they threatened him. Because he had named some of them, he was in danger of being attacked, so the guards isolated him within the jail to protect his life.

Musabyimana made his admissions two years before the law encouraging confession was declared. Later a presidential decree freed him, and he returned to his home area after ten years in prison. There the local community shunned him. He opened a small shop to survive, but his fellow Hutus avoided him, and only survivors purchased from him. Observing the Tutsis' humanity, he came to realize that his grandmother's opinions about them were wrong.

When Musabyimana had the opportunity to attend a healing workshop, he put himself in the position of the survivors and decided to speak out about what he had done. "I repented, apologized and began to weep in sorrow for my deeds." After his confession, Buhanda, a survivor, stood and announced, "I forgive you for what you have confessed." Because Musabyimana had killed Buhanda's sister, his words of acceptance relieved him of much inner pain.

Buhanda, the quiet, diminutive survivor, then told me how Musabyimana had contributed to the death of nine of his family members and how, with others, he had beaten Buhanda, cutting his forehead and the back of his head. While he lay unconscious, they hacked his Achilles tendon and left him to die.

Buhanda & Musabyimana   © John Steward

Though Buhanda survived, his many injuries required regular hospital treatments that he could not afford, and so he suffered much.

When Musabyimana returned from prison, Buhanda's physical pain had lessened, but his emotional trauma lingered because he was consumed with anger. When he first heard Musabyimana confess his deeds in the healing workshop, it was a terrible moment for him. Buhanda was determined to do what he could so that Rwanda would never again be threatened by genocide. When he learned that Hutus had shunned Musabyimana, he offered his friendship. "We survivors are very poor," he said, "as are those released from prison. General poverty is creating a sorrowful life. It is not easy to reconcile when there are such problems, because it is easier to blame the other. If we can solve poverty, then reconciliation will speed up." When Musabyimana declined an invitation to a wedding because his clothes were like rags, Buhanda took him to the market and purchased some suitable clothes for him. "He has become one of my best friends in life," Musabyimana said. "We share whatever we have. When I legalized my marriage, he was my groomsman."

In 2007, Musabyimana went before the gacaca courts. He was sentenced to twenty-five years in jail, which was halved due to his truth-telling. Because he had already spent ten years in jail, the balance of his sentence was commuted to two years of community work. He began at once to make reparation. As a carpenter, he offered his services at no charge to help rebuild houses that had been destroyed during the genocide, making a window for one survivor and a door for the house of another. He continued:

> The healing of our relationship can benefit the whole of Rwanda. I go to many places with Buhanda to tell people about our reconciliation. People see the two of us going everywhere, and they say, "What has happened to these two people?" I am still haunted by the memories of what I did, especially when I walk past the broken and empty houses. I wish I could give back all that was lost in this country. I can't, but I will do what I can. I want to rebuild Rwanda to the limit of my strength.

In 2012 Buhanda said, "I live in a country where a person who did harm to me now lives in harmony with me. My first harvest was getting out of hatred." He said that it had been difficult to learn to live with the people who had brought such harm, but the government was training survivors to welcome their former enemies in order to rebuild the society and to bring an end to the divisions. Putting his arm around Musabyimana, he commented, "It has gone beyond friendship. It is like brotherhood. We want to tell our story. We want the world to know about our reconciliation after conflict."

Mukarurinda and Ndayisaba

In November 2007, the filmmaker Dave Fullerton visited Rwanda to capture stories of healing and reconciliation after the first decade of post-genocide healing. Two Rwandan youth assisted us as guides and translators. We filmed those who wanted to tell of their experiences and so inspire others to participate in healing and reconciliation. Mukarurinda and Ndayisaba, two members of UKA, had participated in the gacaca hearings – Mukarurinda as *inyangamugayo* judge, Ndayisaba as perpetrator and confessor.

When we visited Mukarurinda's home, a young lad ran to me, took my hand and led me into the house. Inside, other children received us with a handshake. Mukarurinda's husband, Charles, welcomed me warmly, a gentle giant with a generous face and signs of suffering on his body. In 1994, he had been left for dead and thrown into the river. He showed me a photograph of his father, Rwanda's first agriculturalist, who introduced pyrethrum. Pyrethrum, a natural insecticide which thrives at high altitudes and on volcanic soils in the hills around Ruhengeri, is currently one of Rwanda's small, but increasing, export crops.

As Mukarurinda served bottled drinks, removing the cap in our presence,[5] it dawned on me that the three children she had introduced had all been born since the genocide. I gave them some of the small toys my older granddaughter had gathered for children in Rwanda and offered an Australian souvenir cloth to Mukarurinda to hang on the wall as a reminder that people far from her country were inspired by her life. When she learned that I only had daughters, she put her hand on their youngest boy and gently said, "He can be the son you didn't have." Such generosity often marked those whose pain was being healed and whose energy was being released for others.

When we began filming, Mukarurinda confidently told her story. In 1994 she was in the crowd of several thousand, hoping to find shelter in the Ntarama church, when the army arrived on buses to supplement the militia and they began to slaughter everyone. Most of her relatives were killed, but she climbed over the high wire fence with her baby and caught her breath in the nearby banana plantation. Then she ran some kilometres to the marshes, where they hid for a month. During that time, she was separated from her husband. When the militia found her, they attacked and killed her baby, hacked at Mukarurinda, severed her hand, and left her unconscious.

For a long time after being rescued by soldiers, her body was paralyzed, and she lived in one of the houses emptied by the exiles. "I wanted to avoid people and to be closer to God," she said. Beginning in 2000, the idea of forgiveness began to grow in her. She built friendships with both Hutu and Tutsi and began to treat them as one family, because she realized Tutsis had not been massacred by the whole population of Rwanda, but just certain people. She attended a healing workshop, began to lead small groups and joined in the community development work of UKA. Mukarurinda was

---

5. Opening beverages in front of the person became important after 1994, when poisoning of drinks became a favourite form of revenge for some.

chosen as an *inyangamugayo* in the local gacaca court. After seeing many perpetrators confess to their crimes and witnessing the power of forgiveness during the hearings, she longed for someone to confess to attacking her. But no one did.

One day, as she was helping some UKA members build a house for a survivor, a young man named Ndayisaba, who was also volunteering, came and knelt before her, crying out, "Mukarurinda, please forgive me, please forgive me." His blubbering took her by surprise and made no sense to her. He had been in the same healing workshop as her and had been quiet throughout, so she told him to go home, calm down and come back to talk another day. The next day he returned and said, "I am the one who attacked you and left you for dead. I can keep my secret no longer." Mukarurinda was moved to forgive him because he was telling the truth and had already started making restitution for the deaths of others he killed by building houses for those made homeless by the genocide.

Ndayisaba, who had sat pensively on her left while we filmed her story, now spoke up. First he pointed to another woman, seated on his left, and indicated that he had killed her five children. He then turned to his right and pointed to the stump of Mukarurinda's right arm and the wound on her head and said, "I did that too." He said that even though he had been helped by the healing workshop, he had not been able to tell the truth or apologize for a long time. "It was a struggle for me to ask for forgiveness. In my heart I was willing, but my tongue was unable to confess." After he confessed to Mukarurinda, and to others whose family members he killed, they began to share meals as family; he felt liberated and free. When it came to the time for his gacaca hearings Ndayisaba confessed his deeds against Mukarurinda and others, served his commuted seven-year prison sentence, and then was released with the desire to inspire others to confess to their crimes.

The following day, we filmed a group of UKA members building a house for a survivor. Mukarurinda sat in the shade while sweat poured off Ndayisaba in the mid-morning sun as he pushed wet clay in between the mud and straw bricks, making visible the work of restitution. Mukarurinda was radiant. Ndayisaba was thoughtful, determined and quiet. He had faced judgement by telling the truth and had been set free from guilt. Now, he offered generosity instead of inflicting pain, and shared in the costly but satisfying work of reconstruction. We were just across the road from the Nyamata church, where 45,000 bodies and artifacts lay in haunting underground crypts.

When we left the construction site to film at the Ntarama Church Genocide Memorial, Ndayisaba and Mukarurinda asked to accompany us. As we walked through the church and observed the clothes of victims hanging from the walls, tears came to Mukarurinda's eyes. "This is the first time I have been back in this awful place since it happened," she said. "I have not been here for over thirteen years." She added that because of the gift of Ndayisaba's apology, she had strength to return to the place where her painful nightmare began. As we drove away from the memorial, I watched in awe as Mukarurinda and Ndayisaba conversed, bearing witness to a Rwanda healing miracle.[6]

Mukarurinda, John & Ndayisaba   © John Steward

Saverina and Karinda

We filmed Saverina, a middle-aged widow, in her simple, unadorned rural home, which was set high on a grassy hillside to the east of Kigali, overlooking

---

6. This story of reconciliation shaped three video segments: "Ntarama Church Massacre", "In the Marshes" and "Building Peace". They are posted on the Rwandan stories website (www.rwandanstories.org) and have been used by teachers and students in classrooms around the world.

silvery Lake Muhazi. We sat around a small table in the tiny, dim front room. The creaking of the tin roof in the glow of the mid-morning sun tapped out the news that it was warming up outside.

Saverina began:

> Before the 1994 genocide we lived in a harmonious community. We were not suspicious of each other nor did we think anything could come between us. We borrowed things, we gave each other brides, we attended weddings, and we did community work together. So when things started to change, we still thought we would be safe. We did not suspect anything bad would happen.

When the carnage commenced in her area, they started with her husband's brother. Then her husband fled, and many other people ran, but Saverina could not run anywhere with seven young children. Once the destroyers started looting their household, she moved the children into a neighbour's house, but they were soon found. They said, "We are going to kill only boys and men; we will spare the girls and women." They took her three boys, and she remained in that home with her three daughters and one adopted daughter.

But they brought her sons back, because someone had pleaded for their lives. Later, they returned again and took the boys to a place where the community had gathered to watch. "That is how I lost my boys," Saverina said. After losing her husband, three sons and extended family in the genocide, life seemed hopeless, and Saverina tried to commit suicide in nearby Lake Muhazi.

After the RPF came to liberate the area, they asked for help in identifying those who had participated in the massacre. They took the accused to prison, but Saverina did not know who had killed her boys. Several years later, the youth who had participated were given amnesty and released to return home, with little warning or preparation. In the uneasy calm, no one came to Saverina to confess.

Then one day, a young man reappeared in the village. After some weeks, he came to Saverina's house to ask if he could accompany her to church. It was several kilometres away, and they walked together in silence. After the service, they returned without a word being said. Saverina realized he might have something to tell her, so as they reached her home, she suggested, "Why don't you come and visit me this week and bring one or two of your friends with you?" She thought this might give him courage. That week, he returned with a friend and confessed to slaughtering one of her children.

Saverina now signalled for the young man sitting beside her to speak. Karinda began hesitantly, with furrowed brow:

> When the war started I ran with the mob, looking for people. We were a large group. We entered various homes. One day, we were sitting in a bar down in the central area and someone called to us – "Saverina's children are here – let's kill them." My group found Saverina's family hiding in an old man's home, along with many others. The adults in the group told us, "You younger ones must kill these children. We are not going to have their blood on our hands." So we boys all shared in attacking them. I and another lad killed one of them. Afterwards, I felt restless, guilty and helpless. I lost my peace. I was sick and I slept a lot.
>
> The RPF came and told those who had been involved to confess publicly and seek forgiveness so they could start life again. I remained silent and moved away to live in another area. But wherever I went, I had no peace. In the end, I decided to go home, even if it meant they'd kill me just as I killed those children.

Karinda explained how, shortly after his return, a man accused him of killing a person he did not even know. The man reported him to the authorities and Karinda spent the next three years in jail. He had constant nightmares, and he could not stop thinking about the killing of the children. When the authorities discovered the man had falsely accused Karinda, they released him. Although he was free, he had no peace. He could neither eat, nor farm, and he did not know what he was doing with his life. Eventually, he decided that he had to confess, even if it meant returning to prison or being killed in revenge. He began to look for an opportunity to tell Saverina that he had helped to kill her sons.

"I walked with her to church but could not open my mouth," he admitted. "When I finally got the courage to confess and apologize, she forgave me." Because Saverina was ready to forgive Karinda, their relationship was transformed from estrangement to acceptance. Each time he came to the house, he was faced with the absence of Saverina's sons. Karinda continued with difficulty, "I can't bring back her children, but I can do some of the things they would do for her, if they were here. I have been coming each week to do odd jobs for her, like cutting the hedges, finding fodder for her animal, cleaning out the cow shed, and fetching water."

Annie Kaligirwa, project coordinator from the Episcopal Commission of Justice and Peace (ECJP), worked extensively with Karinda and Saverina, and she shared her insights about the wider significance of their restored relationship and fruitful partnership:

> They are a model for other people who are wondering about asking forgiveness or being asked to forgive. In our ECJP workshops, Saverina and Karinda often stand up together and tell their story. The workshops do not emphasize justice, but on the deep feelings of hurt – and how you feel when you ask for forgiveness, and when you forgive. These are the essential parts of the process, which bring about life changes.
>
> Saverina has gone on to help others face their own trauma and understand forgiveness as a process. Many people who ask for forgiveness are not forgiven at the moment of asking, because forgiveness is a journey, which takes time.
>
> To forgive a person and be reconciled with them does not mean I must remain their best friend or even must remain in contact with them. But in close-knit communities, individuals cannot move away, so estranged people have to learn how to work together for the community.

Karinda's restitution   © Dave Fullerton

Annie later informed us that Saverina, who served as one of the *inyangamugayo* (wise people) in the gacaca, actively encouraged people to penitence, while Karinda modelled his change of heart by helping Saverina with gardening and maintenance. He was also part of the group who built a house for her, the one in which we were sitting to record them. Annie continued:

> In gacaca, in the decisions handed down by the judges, reparation was compulsory. Yet Saverina and Karinda voluntarily chose a cooperative response. Many stories of prisoners who were given early release tell how they sought out the survivors of those they had killed, and whose possessions they had stolen, and began to

work the land of their victims without expectation of personal economic benefit. This kind of pro-active behaviour is reparation at its best.

Saverina and Karinda showed others a way of living in healthy relationship across both ethnic and generational divides. Saverina demonstrated to adults how they could listen to youth telling their stories. And because of Karinda's example, other young people in the community who participated in the killings began to confess and ask forgiveness.

Over time, Saverina forgave twenty-five young men – those who killed her children and those who stole her property. She also adopted an orphan boy into her family. In Saverina's and Karinda's story, reconciliation, forgiveness and unity became tangible and attainable. This is not only an example for Rwanda, but for all parts of the world in conflict.

Saverina & Karinda embrace © Dave Fullerton

After Gacaca

After the gacaca proceedings officially ended in 2010, Munyeli continued to be involved in promoting healing and peacebuilding programs throughout Rwanda. In a conversation we had during this time, she noted that meaningful re-integration remains one of the great challenges for Rwanda: "For some, gacaca was merely a way to get out of jail. Yet gacaca was founded on the hope of restoring the accused, when possible, to life in the community. For though one of the long-term goals of gacaca was reconciliation, in reality many communities remain divided – coexisting peacefully, but not speaking to one another."

In spite of the gacaca hearings, many Rwandans never had the opportunity to talk about their stories – even after twenty years. Munyeli observed: "When the memorial month comes each April, many survivors have flashbacks. The feelings re-surface as they remember the trauma of past days, they re-imagine people coming to kill them, they see grenades being thrown, and they see people destroying their homes. Some take revenge, others commit suicide."

Ex-prisoners also experience the trauma, particularly those who participated as children in the genocide and were released from prison without assistance or penalty, because they were minors at the time. But without any opportunity for healing, those children now have many unresolved problems. And gacaca did not help all Rwandans deal with the issues they had to face after the genocide. As Munyeli observed:

> Before 1994 I didn't know of a single case of cancer. But now many people have it. Maybe it's because of trauma and all the bad things that happened or it might be because of the weapons that were used around in the country. We don't know exactly why there is such a high level of cancer now.
>
> Trauma means that there is something that affects our brain, or our heart, probably both. People who have trauma find its effects are so heavy compared to the emotional strength they used to have. So for people to heal trauma, they need to bring out the stories and memories that are in their hearts and minds and to talk about them. Otherwise, they can't heal. They need to be opened, to have 'surgery', so that their bodies can accept what they went through and decide what to do with that.
>
> It starts with acceptance, accepting that I am traumatized and that I am dealing with some terrible issues inside of me. Unfortunately, people who are traumatized don't know this or they deny it. They bury it inside. Once they take a step to accept and say, "Yes, I have suffered, yes I have pain, then what . . . ?" This is the beginning of change.

Munyeli offered an insightful view about why we find it so hard to face our inner pain, unravel our many emotions and find the desire to do the work that will lead to personal transformation:

> In the process of healing, when you accept your pain, you have to allow yourself the consequence of the pain, because pain is heavy. Pain destroys our feelings, pain destroys our thinking, and we have to know that we are destroyed and allow ourselves to be destroyed, to be broken. We have to accept that we are broken, to allow our body and our feelings to be broken. And once we

feel the brokenness, we can cry, and we can share, and we have started a journey.

After brokenness it is a long process. We feel that we are not okay. When we are not okay, we have to do something to be okay. We have to have pity on ourselves and say, "We need to live," to embrace life, and to believe we have a future. And once we start to realize that we have to live, despite what happened, and despite what is around us, we can start forgiving. After forgiving ourselves, we start to see the reasons why we have to live. And when we decide that, the trauma heals.

The inner conflict unites both victims and the perpetrators; whether they want to admit it or not, they are connected by violence. For the perpetrator, there is guilt and shame, not being able to forgive themselves for what they did, being full of hatred. For the victim, the main feelings are anger, sadness, shame and grief, and so they avoid contact, become bitter and seek revenge.

Neither side is at peace. The healing process works to re-humanize both groups.

Munyeli made her comments about cancer and healing during the filming of her experiences as a leader of healing, a trainer and pioneer in the preparations for gacaca, and as one who attended her local weekly gacaca hearings. She believed that her observations about pain and brokenness applied to any person who struggled with an unresolved painful past, whether in Africa or beyond.

Beyond Rwandan Borders

Using a combination of film, photography and journalism, Dave Fullerton compiled twenty short video stories of Rwanda, as told through the eyes of survivors and perpetrators. Dave's wife, Sally Morgan, developed the *Vanishing Point* curriculum package to accompany the short films.[7] She and other classroom teachers tested the material in secondary classrooms in Australia for teachers of English, history, geography, civics, health, law and

---

7. All of the materials can be viewed and accessed on the website www.rwandanstories.org. The educational materials, including lessons, handouts, assessment pages, training guidelines and videos can also be purchased on USB.

social studies, as well as peace and reconciliation courses. Dozens of secondary students around the world have since engaged with the curriculum.

The United Nations Association of Australia awarded Rwandanstories. org "The Best Online Peace Media for 2011". The judges were particularly impressed with the humanitarian focus of the web site, which sets the genocide in both historical and contemporary contexts. They also appreciated the way the site "aims to answer some of the big picture questions about how genocide begins, what sort of society makes an event like this possible, and how society can start to possibly recover from such an event." The curriculum draws on numerous primary sources to provide an accessible exploration of tolerance, resilience, the human inclination towards prejudice, and the need for building a peaceful society. The stunning visual material with powerful human-interest stories has attracted attention of teachers and secondary students from 190 countries.

At the end of 2012, I visited Rwanda to update the stories for this book and to say "thank you" to the Rwandans we had filmed. The films revealed to them how their words and stories were being received around the world, and their tears of joy reminded me that education is an important aspect of restitution. Though the wider world had looked the other way during the terrible events of 1994, they were now paying attention to the dignity and hope that was returning to Rwandans who had looked their painful past in the face and found reasons to live with new resolves and deeper courage.

It was important for youth in Rwanda to witness the return of dignity and hope through healing, forgiveness and reconciliation. As the younger generation they needed to find a way to lament the troubling history they inherited and acknowledge the damaging trauma that their relatives and neighbours had experienced. They had to find a new way forward if they were to have a future. In Part 6: *Facing the Future*, I turn to the stories of how some youth in Rwanda contributed to healing, restoration and change in their country, post-genocide.

6

Facing the Future

"Those who were fighting are now dancing together!"
A prisoner, Gitarama

A Dream for Youth: Rutimburana

During my first months in Rwanda, I had visited colleagues in different areas of the country so that I might understand the distinctive challenges within each region.

North of Kigali, Byumba is the nearest Rwandan highway exit to Uganda. Mountainous, misty and cold, the region is known for its tea plantations – neatly trimmed, refreshing green bushes stretching away from the main road. This is where Munyeli and her boys found refuge in the emergency camp, which was established while the war for Rwanda raged between the RPF and the Rwandan army/Hutu militia until July 1994.

In Byumba, Rutimburana, our NGO area manager for the region, told me about his experience as a boy, fleeing Rwanda through Byumba to Uganda in 1961, escaping a Hutu who was brandishing a knife at him. He had lived in exile in Uganda for thirty-three years, where he and his family had experienced constant discrimination and poverty. Now that he was back in the homeland he wanted youth to have new opportunities.

As a teacher for many years, Rutimburana knew how negatively youth had been affected by the cycles of killing since the late 1950s, which had culminated with the genocide. He believed that those in power in Rwanda before 1994 had instilled the hatred between Hutu and Tutsi, and he dreamed of educating youth and inviting them to live an alternative story of reconciliation and peace. He hoped to engage youth and invite them to share their hopes for reconciliation through essay competitions, public debates, art and cartooning, sports, income generation, and visits to genocide sites. I was impressed with the clarity of his vision.

Shortly after the government began urging NGOs to take action with the many Rwandan youth who had been separated from their families in the chaos and dislocation after the genocide. Were these youth vulnerable to being recruited as child soldiers by the rebel groups in Congo, who wanted to complete the genocide, or could they instead bring their survival skills to help build a new Rwanda?

Reaching Unaccompanied Youth

On Easter Sunday 1997, a day shadowed by the sombre third anniversary of the genocide, Sandi and I drove south from Kigali to Nyamata, past the marshes of the Bugesera swamp where, unlike many others, Mukarurinda had hidden and survived. Along with a Canadian NGO executive who was interested in the future of Rwandan youth, we visited a hapless mix of three hundred unaccompanied children, who did not know of a single living relative with whom they could live. These children had all survived daunting challenges to accessing the basic necessities of food, water, clothes and shelter for over two years.

A few of the braver children slowly came forward for 'sides together right,' a game of two pairs of open hands connecting in a high-five clap.

Nyamata children & Sandi   © John Steward

The cautious, uncertain faces and shy looks of the children was gradually transformed into laughter as child after child ran back to the end of the queue, awaiting the next opportunity to exchange a brief touch and smile with Sandi, the gentle *muzungu*.

On the return drive to Kigali, my guest said, "These resilient children are Rwanda's future. I wonder what their contribution will be to the building of peace in this country." As our weaving vehicle alternately avoided and hit deep potholes, I shared Rutimburana's hopes for using art as a way for the youth to express their dreams for a peaceful future. Though Rwanda was a troubled, gloomy society, I observed how creativity and energy had emerged during celebrations that had used cultural forms of expression – drums, clapping, dancing and storytelling. We also talked about how art, drama, singing, prose and poetry were being used elsewhere to process trauma among children.

The Canadian offered to seek a donor who could support an arts program that would be developed, initiated and managed by Rwandans. I agreed to outline a program proposal that encouraged youth of mixed ethnicity to develop artistic presentations using art, dance, music, drama and poetry, to highlight their aspirations for a peaceful future in Rwanda. I explained that the full proposal would need to emerge from Rwandans, rather than expatriates, and that this would need time to develop. The fresh memory of so many unaccompanied children in Nyamata stirred me into action.

Accompanying Youth: Ikiriza

Once the start-up funding had been secured, I recruited Ikiriza as project manager, a native Rwandan who loved youth and whose verve, empathy and determination could motivate them to work together, a difficult task in the tension-filled atmosphere of Rwanda at that time. Ikiriza had previous experience advocating on behalf of children throughout the country.

Ikiriza's compassion for dislocated children and struggling youth stemmed from her own childhood. Her mother had died when she was six months old, and an aunt in Uganda adopted her. When she was ten years old, her adoptive family was forced to return to Rwanda. During her time in refugee camps, she saw children of all ages suffering and dying, and from a very young age, she dedicated herself to serving children living in difficult circumstances. Later, because Ikiriza did not know sufficient French to attend school in Rwanda, she returned to Uganda to study in English. As an orphan, she received advice from many members of her extended family (clan), but she was not responsible to anyone in particular. Eventually, when no one stepped forward to pay her school fees, she had to drop out of high school, and Ikiriza took on menial work in Uganda.

After the genocide, a cousin invited Ikiriza to return to Rwanda, where she found work tracing lost children throughout Rwanda and reuniting them with their relatives. In two years, she and her British colleague had placed over a thousand children back into families. This work of tracing links to families and communities reflected the government's desire to avoid opening orphanages. When children could not be placed with a relative, the government planned clusters of homes with adult supervision to help the isolated kids regain some sense of community.

Ikiriza   © Dave Fullerton

In April 1997, the government of Rwanda began to repatriate refugees who were still living in Congo, bringing in eight flights a day from three locations. Among these refugees were 1,074 unaccompanied children. On one day alone, twenty-four children were brought to a transit house at Nyamata, where Ikiriza and others sought to connect each child with a relative. Ikiriza remarked on the condition of the children who reached the transit house:

> They had scratches, cuts and wounds, skin diseases. They looked badly malnourished, wore threadbare clothes, and had swollen feet. One girl had a bullet in her wrist, another could hardly walk. Some of the children had been on their own in the refugee camps or the jungles of Congo for over two years. I wanted these children to have a life and to be able to find their families and be part of reconciliation and establishing right relationships.

When I visited the Nyamata transit house during this influx, I watched these children line up for high-protein biscuits, which they ate with great urgency. As they received a bar of soap, a blanket and sleeping mat, they grasped each object lovingly, and then skipped triumphantly towards their hut.

An hour later, Ikiriza and I bumped over undulating roads to re-connect a thirteen-year-old girl with her family. She had not seen them since their separation in the Congo sometime in the previous two and a half years. Hesitantly, the young lady walked the final three hundred metres of her 600 kilometre journey from home to jungle and back again. Following behind the small group who escorted her, I heard shouts of recognition from the gardens and saw faces appear around the trees that lined the path. Old friends offered hugs and huge smiles. Fifty metres down the track, the girl's two brothers welcomed her. Further down the trail, older people appeared, giving her their greetings. As she reached the clearing in front of the family home, her mother rushed out and embraced her. "Where have you been? How did you get there? How did you get here?" she asked. Then, in a hesitant voice, "Where is your sister?" The girl did not know. The mother wiped away her tears, took a step back from her daughter, looked at those of us who stood watching from the edge of the clearing, opened her arms wide and said, "I have nothing to give you as my thanks, but I place you all before the Almighty."

Ikiriza expressed the privilege she felt in participating in the restoration of this young woman to her family and community. The irony was not lost on her, for as an orphan, she had just reunited one more child with her mother. When I interviewed her for the work of the youth program, Ikiriza stated her commitment to work with youth because they are the future of the nation, are easily swayed, have energy and can be spiritually dynamic. She believed that if youth were trained to become better citizens, it could help break the cycle of violence. She suggested:

> In the past, Rwandan values were shaped by parents, extended family and clan members, which created confusion when the youth were manipulated for political ends in 1994. During the genocide, the energy of many youth was channelled into the destruction of people and property. Only with changed attitudes will this energy be directed to positive developmental thinking and purposeful action. The Rwanda experience shows that if the spiritual and mental aspects are underdeveloped, physical well-being can be quickly destroyed.

Promoting Reconciliation Among Youth (PRAY)

Over the next several months, Ikiriza developed the concept and planned the goals for the Promoting Reconciliation among Youth (PRAY) program. Her focus was to organize young people to work in small groups to promote reconciliation by creating art, dance, poetry, music and drama that illustrated their hopes and dreams for a peaceful Rwanda. PRAY targeted Rwandan youth between the ages of thirteen and twenty-five, as over 40 percent of the Rwandan population fell into this category. The work focused on four zones within Rwanda: Byumba, Gikongoro, Nyamata, Ruhengeri and their surrounding districts. With Ikiriza as the project manager, several assistants eventually joined her. Every six months, I would consult with and mentor Ikiriza and her small team in planning, budgeting, evaluating and reporting. These visits allowed me to monitor the progress of the program and to celebrate the youth's impact on others, particularly adults.

The PRAY pilot project began early in 1998, with an essay competition for several secondary schools in the vicinity of Byumba.[1] Students and teachers gathered to celebrate and present sections of their essays to a public audience, along with traditional songs, original poems, music and dancing. Through the pilot project, Ikiriza learned important aspects of planning and reporting. She also discovered youth's readiness to share ideas for a peaceful Rwanda – and she assessed the public's willingness to gather for the youth presentations. In 1998, reconciliation was not yet on the government agenda and was perceived as premature and controversial among adults. Many people resisted peacebuilding work because it was too confrontational and challenged their beliefs, values, attitudes and behaviour.

The PRAY pilot project indicated that students could work responsibly around themes of forgiveness, reconciliation and justice, using their creative ideas to express hope for an inclusive, peaceful Rwanda. Two principles guided the development of the project. First, we did not want to promote competition, as there was already too much of it in Rwanda, and we knew it could create tension within or between groups and families. Second, we felt that awarding prizes to individuals would not promote acceptance and equality among the participating students and schools. Thus we decided to recognize every participant and offer a practical benefit to each participating school, community or group – such as library books, implements for school gardens or instruments and equipment for classroom or group activities.

For the next three years, Ikiriza travelled widely throughout the four zones to meet with local leaders and visit secondary schools. She found at least one sympathetic teacher within each of forty different schools who was willing to serve as mentor for a group of between twelve and fifteen students, preferably

---

1. The area is now called Gicumbi.

PRAY group rehearsing   © Annet Ikiiriza

with balanced representation of gender and ethnicity. Though students were encouraged to draw on traditional Rwandan concepts about peaceful human relationships, their mandate was to create original material that reflected fresh thinking about healing and new ways of relating peacefully. Each group was to integrate two or more types of traditional artistic expression into a thirty-minute group presentation, choosing from forms such as recitations of prose or poetry, storytelling, music, dancing, drama, mime and art. The time limit enabled groups to perform at civic ceremonies, special events, church services, and weddings.

Ikiriza spoke about the difficulty she faced in overcoming the cultural resistance among adults in their willingness to listen to youth.

> Youth have ideas, concerns and hopes to share with adults. In Rwandan culture, it was not common for youth or children to express themselves in that way. It was always parents telling the youth what was acceptable with their "do's and don'ts". Many youth faced challenges from their parents, who resisted their involvement in a mixed group, which included traditional enemies. Some parents asked, "Why do you want to remind us of all our grief and loss?" The teachers were also impacted, as they were present for discussions that faced questions they had previously avoided.[2]

Ikiriza also interacted with local government, civic and NGO leaders, inviting them to support, promote and attend the presentations by youth.

---

2. This extract comes from Annet Ikiriza, *Voices of Hope* (World Vision Rwanda, 2003), 52.

Some adults feared she was conveying dangerous messages to the youth, but gradually people came to realize the program gave youth a positive outlet to express constructive ideas for a peaceful future in Rwanda. The youth became energized as they worked together, developing plans and plays, props and costumes to increase the effects of their words, dances and songs. Sometimes, their messages were blunt and forceful as they expressed their disappointment with the older generation for drawing much of Rwanda into the events of 1994. Though the presentations reflected great energy and hope, many adults were sober and quiet as they heard the truth being told from the perspective of the youth.

Ikiriza remembered how many times, after seeing the presentations, she was moved to apologize on behalf of adults, because the students showed so clearly how adults involved them in the genocide and were now hindering their healing and reconciliation process. "I cannot remember how many times I shed tears after the youth presented their materials," she said, "because I felt challenged and sad at how much adults had failed the younger generation."

As PRAY developed, the word 'reconciliation' often provoked negative emotions, particularly among local authorities. Leaders often taunted, "Reconciliation between who and who?" Others said, "You are part of an NGO and talking of reconciliation? Who funds this organization? Don't you know how the West failed to care for Rwanda in 1994? Have you been bought out by white foreigners?" We discussed changing the name of the project so that it didn't include the word 'reconciliation', but we chose to stick with the title, face our challengers and keep the discussion going.

Ikiriza's relative, Dorothea, revealed her resistance to PRAY when she said in a public meeting: "All my four sisters, together with their children and mine, were killed in the genocide. I told Ikiriza she was doing the impossible; and I could not reconcile with anybody." Ikiriza persisted in asking her to attend 'just one' of the public youth expositions. Eventually, Dorothea agreed to go and was deeply moved. She said: "When I saw the youth dancing and singing about reconciliation, I realized, if we had been told these things long ago, unity and reconciliation could have been achieved when I was still young. This is the only way I know of preventing any future conflict. These youth gave me a surge of hope for the future of my country and community."

Over time, the youth presentations began to influence local communities, authorities, school directors and teachers. And finally, in 2000, the Rwandan government established the National Unity and Reconciliation Commission (NURC), which placed reconciliation on the national agenda. Slowly, the persistent, negative attitudes of local authorities towards peacebuilding reconciliation efforts softened and changed.

National Youth Convention

Eventually, PRAY groups began to travel into other zones to make their presentations. Since different areas experienced the ethnic tensions and genocide differently, this movement across regions allowed stories and viewpoints from one part of Rwanda to be heard in other parts. The idea emerged to gather youth representatives from all four regions for a national convention to share their presentations and learn from one another. At the same time, Ikiriza could gather feedback to plan for the future of the project.

In 2001, 120 youth gathered in Kigali for one week, along with twenty international visitors, including the project donors and some media. A packed audience filled the National Cultural Centre for the public opening ceremony, which was filmed for the evening TV news. The impressive ceremony abounded with laughter, fun and youthful energy expressed in well-rehearsed recitation, dance, drama, and music, interspersed with several speeches by government, donors and civic leaders. The Minister of Youth, Sports and Culture spoke in favour of the project. Delphina expressed the relief that came to her in forgiving Bembereza and his offer of restitution (a story recounted in Part 5: *Judging for Justice*).

During the week the youth attended educational sessions on the role of drama in communicating messages, and using mindful meditation to maintain inner quiet. They also participated in small group discussions that challenged them to dream of their role in shaping the future and to explore how to be aware and to respond to the women who were abused during the genocide and suffered in the ensuing HIV/AIDS epidemic. The donors were so impressed with the project's scope and significance that they agreed to continue funding for a further three years.

At the end of the convention, the youth created and presented their summary statement:

> We, the group of 120 Rwandan youth, are a mixture of students, non-students and child-headed households, who are committed to promoting peace and reconciliation in our communities. During this convention we shared our messages with many audiences – including in the prisons of Butare and Gitarama. Different facilitators helped us in plenary sessions addressing

issues that concern us. After knowing clearly the role of the youth in the reconciliation process, we wish to thank the government of Rwanda for putting reconciliation into their priorities by forming the NURC. We also thank the project donors and facilitators for providing an opportunity for the youth to speak out. We thank church leaders for reminding Rwandans to be at peace with each other. We thank the Canadians for giving the funds for this project.

They concluded by making four commitments to their role in shaping Rwanda's future: "We promise all Rwandans we will give constructive ideas. We will use our energy to rehabilitate people and property. We want to take a leading role in the reconciliation process wherever we are. We will continue to be a living example to our parents, younger sisters and brothers."

Youth Reach Out to Prisoners

Two teams from the convention travelled south to make presentations to several thousand prisoners at two prisons. I accompanied the group to Gitarama prison. We sat looking at a huge, densely packed group in pink prison garb, who were gathered in the heat of the noonday sun in the square brick courtyard. Many more prisoners peered out from behind the bars of windows in the three-story building that formed the back and sides of the courtyard.

The prison director welcomed us and announced that his prison had an 11 percent confession rate – the lowest among the thirteen prisons of Rwanda, where the confession rate averaged 20 percent. The presence of *muzungus* was an occasion for the authorities to remind inmates that "The whole world is watching Rwanda to see how it will resolve the problem of our over-crowded prisons."

Sweating and straining to see over and around one another, the audience watched the youth troupe. The well-rehearsed dances were energetic, acrobatic and humorous – but also pointed. Hutu and Tutsi, male and female, danced together, alternately swaying towards each other, then withdrawing, symbolizing a history the prisoners knew well. The dance brought diverse reactions from the crowd – amazement and embarrassment, smiles and frowns.

The group sang a song they had written about truth, reconciliation and accountability. The inmates gasped when they quoted two Rwandan proverbs: "The stone damaged the hoe – we need another stone to straighten it" and "The same person who caused the problem is the one to heal it." Then, fourteen-year-old Charlotte Mukantwali looked slowly around at the wall of two thousand faces, pulled a toy gun from her belt, fired it in the air, threw it over her shoulder and recited:

> Peace doesn't come through the barrel of a gun.
> We need peace, but reconciliation must come before peace.
> Rwanda my country, what happened to you?
> Before, we were all united and we helped each other, but we are
>   now divided.
> Though we had been breast-fed together this did not last
>   because of those who were selfish and forgot our culture
>   and divided us.[3]
> I witnessed much, I saw people who had become inhuman, I
>   saw those who became like animals, I saw people hunted
>   down like birds.
> But now we need a spirit of telling the truth – we expect the
>   gacaca tribunals to punish the criminals according to law,
>   for innocent people to be released from prison and then for
>   us all to live together in peace.
> Let's extend peace to each other, and build a culture of peace in
>   our country.
> Youth – if we all stand up together for this, we shall win.

The crowd remained motionless and silent. My translator, who was a prisoner at Gitarama, whispered to me, "These youth have the message that is needed at this time."

Charlotte, who was only seven years old in 1994, represented a new Rwanda, one that courageously confronted adults with the awful significance of their actions, and then looked towards a different future, where youth would lead the way. One of the two thousand faces in the courtyard that day belonged to Charlotte's father. Arrested four years before, he had yet to be charged. Charlotte longed for the truth to come out so that he would be freed. Afterwards, Charlotte explained, "I want the truth to come out – truth means hope. Performing gives me hope, so I want to do as much of it as I can. If all

---

3. The reference is to Hutu and Tutsi mothers nursing their babies while they sat side-by-side. An image of peace!

youth can get involved in this kind of process, then reconciliation is possible. Truth is the main weapon. There must be no more lies about what happened."

On the return bus trip to Kigali, our mini-bus reverberated with the sound of energetic youth singing, pouring out their music with loud drumbeats to those walking along the roadside. I sat next to Ngabo, a prison chaplain, who for seven years had worked among prisoners, bringing groups from outside the prison to visit. I asked for his impression of the day:

> I often take choirs into prisons for Sunday service. Today I realized that a choir is too gentle, too soft for hardened men. These youth gave it to them straight. It was like a smack in the face. It hurt. These prisoners have not heard the truth like this, ever. They realized the youth not only know what they did, but they reject it as a model for themselves. The group actually said, "You older ones gave us a bad example, now please step aside and let us do what is right for the future of this country."

While my group was at the Gitarama prison, another group visited the Butare prison. At the youth convention the next day, one of the youth in the other group announced:

> My mum has been saying for months, "You have to forgive the man who killed your father and siblings. He's probably dead anyway." Yesterday I saw him in the Butare prison. He did not recognize me, but I was instantly troubled. That man attacked me with a screwdriver – and for seven years, every time I've seen a screwdriver, I have picked it up and thrown it as far away as possible. I couldn't sleep because I was haunted by the realization I know I will see him again (during the gacaca justice process).
>
> What was I to do? After thinking about it all night I decided to forgive him. I have let go of my bitterness and my desire for revenge.

She sat and wept for fifteen minutes as Ikiriza consoled her. Later, Ikiriza commented on the challenge of forgiveness and confession: "It is difficult to offer forgiveness to someone who hurt you; it's like putting your finger into a bleeding wound." While some outside observers expressed concern about events, which seem to re-traumatize people, our psychologist colleague Ndogoni explained: "It is better to deal with trauma than suppress it. Every time I feel the inner pain, it is a sign I can do more work for my healing.

Every time I tell my story the pain lessens. And without healing forgiveness is impossible."

PRAY Impacts the Participants

During the youth convention in Kigali, the participants met in small groups to respond to three questions. First, they discussed what PRAY had achieved for peace in Rwanda and what Rwandan youth could do to promote peace in Rwanda. They also compiled a list of the help and support youth needed from the government, NGOs, churches and society. Second, they discussed the feelings, knowledge, attitudes, habits and healing that PRAY evoked in their group? They also talked about people who had seen their performances and how they had been affected. Third, they discussed new ideas and dreams that they would take back to their local PRAY group as well as anything significant, challenging or life changing from their time at the convention.

Based on the feedback from convention participants, Ikiriza's team identified seven desirable outcomes to describe the progress of peacebuilding and reconciliation among youth in Rwanda. These were behavioural markers, which the youth described in their lives as a result of participating in PRAY. In order to determine meaningful criteria for measuring the work of something as intangible as 'peace', 'healing' or 'reconciliation', we accepted the perceptions of the individual who was assessing his or her personal experience. Thus what is experienced subjectively indicates how a person is at that time.[4] The following is a summary of some of the responses of the youth at the convention.

First, youth participants indicated that their emotional wounds had been healed and they had been released from heavy emotions that they had been holding within. Some of the responses indicating shifts in this behavioural marker included: "We have learned to solve our own problems"; "Before I joined in PRAY I had trauma but now I live at peace with myself, as well as those who oppressed me"; "Before I joined I was so sad that I couldn't talk to anybody, now I have some stability and love in my heart."

Second, youth demonstrated changed attitudes and values. They also indicated that they were in relationships that built up people. Some responses indicating changes for this behavioural marker included: "I have confidence

---

4. Known as 'phenomenology', this assumes that whatever someone experiences at a particular moment is real – as real as any object that the person can see, touch or taste. Extracted from Appendix 5 of Ikiriza, *Voices of Hope*, 78.

we can say we are Hutu or Tutsi without any fear or feeling guilty"; "I have now gained a spirit of forgiveness after a long time when I was unable to forgive those who killed my relatives"; "PRAY helps me to have a loving and forgiving heart, and has helped our group join together"; "In our efforts, I used to say that reconciliation was only needed by the genocide perpetrators, but after I joined PRAY I realized that it is for us all"; "We changed our bad behaviour of not talking to others on the grounds that they were Tutsi or Hutu"; "I realized every Rwandan person has the same human rights."

Third, youth began to take action together and to call other people to be reconciled. Responses indicating changes for this behavioural marker included: "Slowly people started to understand our message"; "PRAY has helped some prisoners to tell the truth and to ask for forgiveness"; "For three years we had not been very cooperative in high school, but the last year when we've been part of this project, has been wonderful"; "We are now a group that teach unity without discrimination."

Fourth, youth developed personal integrity through truth sharing and a sense of wholeness. Responses indicating changes for this behavioural marker included: "Even among us there were ethnic divisions – unity and reconciliation has to start among ourselves"; "I joined thinking it was only a matter of singing and acting, but after a while I was impacted"; "We are going to act like mirrors to other youth who haven't had this chance of learning"; "I realize by telling the truth about what we saw during the genocide we can reach peace."

Fifth, youth began to reject divisions in favour of unity. Responses indicating changes for this behavioural marker included: "Parents would come and ask us to include their children in our group"; "Whenever we did our drama people around us discouraged us from saying that unity in Rwanda is possible after the tragedy"; "Because of our drama people have started talking to those they had been avoiding"; "We are all Rwandans"; "As youth we have to forgive without discrimination"; "I never thought I could sit with a Tutsi in the same group, since I am a Hutu"; "I used to feel guilty whenever Tutsi came near me, but after being in the PRAY group I realized they haven't any problems with me."

Sixth, youth began to embrace the process to promote reconciliation. Responses indicating changes for this behavioural marker included: "Involvement in PRAY taught us what we can do in order not to repeat the mistakes of the past"; "I will take an initiative in forgiving and ask for forgiveness"; "We had fear about who we would introduce in the content of our drama because they considered us as enemies"; "Our group will organize an event where we will invite government authorities and schools to show them what we learned through PRAY"; "Reconciliation is a process, so it needs self sacrifice if we are to accept being abused, being hated (for promoting it)."

Seventh, youth became part of a grassroots attitude and movement that challenged negative influences. Responses indicating changes for this behavioural marker included: "Most people who have seen us in action have changed and try to live in peace"; "I learned how to share ideas with different people from different places"; "At weddings we dance and give teachings about unity and reconciliation"; "PRAY helped us connect with youth from other communes and share our message with them"; "Now I know my role as a youth in building a culture of peace"; "Our audience had lost hope for tomorrow, but they changed their minds after hearing us perform"; "After hearing our messages parents allowed their children outside to play"; "When there is an opportunity in our commune to give out peace messages, the authorities call us to perform"; "According to the local officials the message we gave through our drama was more effective than their speeches!"

Many of the youth indicated that they had to change their attitudes and behaviours in order to remain involved with PRAY. One said, "I have had to do away with using some terminology that hurts my Hutu colleagues. I even gained strength to face those who killed my family members." The youth who participated in the convention returned to their local groups with new confidence, eager to report on their experiences, inspire fellow PRAY members, and become agents of peace in their schools, homes and communities.

Rwanda's Vulnerable Youth

The convention evaluations also identified needs that were not being met among vulnerable groups of youth, particularly child-headed households. Following is the story of sixteen-year-old Chantelle, who was responsible for feeding and caring for her younger siblings. Like thousands of other Rwandan youth, Chantelle found herself caring for her household in 1994, when her parents were massacred and she suddenly became the oldest living relative in her family.

Several years after the genocide, her orphaned family could not return to farm her family's plot, because they were afraid they would be attacked by the people who had killed her parents. A relative loaned them land and a small cement house, and Chantelle cultivated this land with her sisters. Though the family had neighbours living within earshot, people left them alone, except when they were asked to work in exchange for beans or corn.

One of Chantelle's sisters still suffered from a hatchet wound in the top of her head and was plagued by headaches. Another child shivered with malaria. To keep warm, she wrapped herself in the red and yellow cloth that Chantelle had just used to cushion her head for the heavy water container she'd carried home from the local water source.

An NGO gave Chantelle monthly rations of rice and dried beans, milk powder, salt, cooking oil and soap. But these items were insufficient for such vulnerable families, and as drought came to the area, fresh food became scarce. If Chantelle could not grow, forage or barter for commodities, her family would go without. Chantelle seemed subdued and fatigued by the constant and demanding work, yet she took her responsibilities seriously, striving to provide food and fetch water for her siblings, even though it meant she could not go to school. Though of marriageable age, she said she would only marry if her prospective husband accepted responsibility for her entire family – something she knew would be unlikely.

Though she felt shame in being uneducated and poor, her deepest cause of discomfort was her failure to locate the bones of her parents. If she could find their remains and give them a proper burial, her sadness would diminish and she could feel peace. Like Chantelle, thousands of other Rwandan youth were living a vulnerable, fragile existence – with no regular income, no schooling and no mature help to fall back on. In response, PRAY agreed to work more closely with child-headed households, particularly the eldest teens, who were carrying personal trauma along with crushing responsibilities and with little support. With the assistance of a psychologist experienced in art therapy, the PRAY team ran healing workshops for fifty-six members of child-headed households. They spent several days re-visiting the pain, understanding and celebrating their resilience, discussing memories of their family and gaining insight into what they had been able to hold from their heritage.

By portraying their lives in drawings, these children shared their painful past with one another. At the beginning, their artwork used strong colours, such as black and red, and they spoke of the 'darkness' of war, 'blood' and 'haunting memories'. In later sessions, they began to use other colours, such as white (to symbolize hope), yellow (to symbolize happiness) and green (to symbolize peace). Rwandan proverbs that mentioned children were another source of nourishment for these traumatized children. Their favourite sayings

Do we knew son-consciously

included: "Another person's child cannot please you"; "Orphans can hear things in the midst of great noise"; "The heart of an orphan develops grey hair before the head of an old man"; "A child who always cries is never rescued".

By drawing together children from child-headed households, PRAY hoped to create local awareness of this vulnerable group and to link the struggling youth with available resources. The PRAY workers became advocates on behalf of the youth to NGOs, government and local survivor associations.

Expanding PRAY's Influence

A month after the convention, one local PRAY group took an initiative to organize a mini-convention at their school, inviting fellow students, teachers, local authorities and community members to hear about their experiences at the convention. The group modified their play to include new issues from the training sessions at the convention, including the education of girls, HIV/AIDS awareness, and the role of the gacaca tribunals.

Because of space limitations, the national convention was restricted to 120 participants. So the following year, Ikiriza arranged two camps for other PRAY groups, accommodating a total of 240 youth. Local authorities covered the cost of these camps and provided accommodation, reflecting a dramatic change in the attitudes of local leaders towards the work of PRAY. When one PRAY group was unable to get a permit to take their drama into a local prison, the mayor obtained permission for them.

These PRAY camps educated youth about cycles of change in a post-genocide society so that they could become involved in the physical and economic development of their communities. Camp participants visited genocide memorial sites to deepen their understanding of the massive destruction and dislocation that their people had suffered. They also reflected on youth's potential contributions to Rwanda's future amidst the challenges of recovery. Youth shared memories of the trauma they had witnessed and experienced during the genocide and processed their emotions upon visiting the memorial sites.

Nineteen-year-old Nyirabuhoro visited the former school where her parents' and sisters' bodies had been stacked, along with 50,000 others. She was shocked when she realized that it would be impossible to identify the remains of her family. For the previous eight years, she had been hoping to find their bodies. At the end of the week, she said, "This PRAY camp was good; it helped my healing. I also learned a lot about gacaca and how to behave towards other people in my community. It is helpful to know about reconciliation. I want to share that with all my friends".

Over time, the initial participants in PRAY graduated from high school, making space for youth who had been waiting for an opportunity to join and also expanding the work of PRAY. Other NGOs also began to focus on youth.

Nyarutovu Youth Day

Early one morning in 2004, I drove with several colleagues to a youth event in the tiny township of Nyarutovu, just outside Ruhengeri. As we drove towards the local sports ground, we passed dozens of youth wearing white T-shirts with the message: "United we Stand". Sitting under a plastic shelter along with local officials and government dignitaries, we listened to the lively chatter, enjoying the colourful clothes as people continued to arrive from the surrounding hills, valleys and distant regions. Much of the crowd of 5,000 had gathered on a slope overlooking the sports field, while latecomers had to stand around the perimeter of the grass. Young boys perched themselves in trees to get a better view. After a few short speeches by district officials and the local youth representative, who stressed the importance of participating in peacebuilding and HIV/AIDS prevention, the next six hours were given over to the youth, who comprised 43 percent of the population of Nyarotovu.

Centre-stage on the sports field, over eight hundred young people from the district had come together to beat drums, perform energetic dances and sing songs of hope, forgiveness, reconciliation and unity. One verse addressed those who had offended, another the guests from outside of their area and a third reminded the youth of their part for building a better future:

> Our friends who committed genocide, understand you have
>   harmed your neighbour,
> But if you can accept your guilt and seek forgiveness we shall
>   forgive you.
> For those who come from afar, you can see for yourself
> We are now sharing everything, we are helping each other.
> Youth, let us refuse any kind of division among us.
> Let unity and reconciliation be our goal!
> Let us promote peace and reconciliation in our communities
> and in our families where we live.

The youth then performed a range of physical activities featuring male and female gymnasts and runners, as well as men's and women's football matches. Though we had debated about the merits of including competitive sports in PRAY events, Ikiriza knew sports would draw youth together to hear reconciliation messages. I had agreed, but objected to football matches, because men in Rwanda dominated football, and I saw it as a symbol of exclusion, not inclusion. For some months, Ikiriza had worked quietly to resolve the dilemma by gathering and training two all-female barefoot teams. I recognized the maturity blossoming in the youth work and congratulated Ikiriza on her creative initiative. To acknowledge the participants, every group received a football, or sports uniforms or hoes. The biggest cheers were for the runners, who received a goat.

Nyarutovu PRAY drama   © Colin Smith

The program also included a gripping drama about ethnic difference and discrimination, which traced a romance across ethnic lines. Amidst tense scenes of irresponsible drunkenness and family arguments, it wove in messages of reconciliation across divides through acts of forgiveness, peace and celebration. As the program ended, the Secretary of the NURC concluded, "Today you have created the condition for our coming together, and when we are together, we can more likely reconcile. Youth, we thank you for what you have done."

As we drove away, dozens of youth, accompanied by smiling adults, skipped along the tarmac, carrying home the blue bags, which held the prizes for their group. The youth glowed with satisfaction, bright faces of Rwanda's future.

Beyond PRAY

As with all foreign-funded projects, the PRAY project came to an end after six years. During the time that PRAY was running, several thousand Rwandan youth created artful presentations to deliver messages of tolerance, forgiveness, peace and reconciliation to an estimated 200,000 adults and young people.

Several years after the youth event in Nyarotovu, Ikiriza reflected on how she had gained trust with the youth by engaging with them on their terms:

> I have had to come down to their level to gain the trust of the youth, but they opened up as a result. I learned to interact in games and discussions with them, forming connections at a level I had never previously experienced. I changed my attitude towards younger people, and discovered that they knew a lot and had dreams and visions they wanted to develop. I opened up to them as well, and learned to admit to them I did not know everything.[5]

Ikiriza's mobilizing work and conversation with the youth taught her that reconciliation was a process, a journey and a possibility that required commitment. She observed that:

> The former leadership of Rwanda took more than thirty years to plan and implement the genocide. In the same way, reconciliation will take time. It is a goal to be reached. We do not know how long it will take in Rwanda, but it is possible. Those who are willing do reconciliation. You cannot wait for the majority to catch the vision. You begin with a few and expand later. It is not done democratically (by the majority), but by the relatively few who are willing and committed.
>
> Reconciliation is not a day job; it is a life which one chooses to live. It goes beyond the workday to include weekends, public holidays and annual leave. One does not do it at an office location but at home, in the kitchen at birthday parties, in conversations at funerals, etc.[6]

Ikiriza noted how reconciliation begins with healing because "a healed heart offers forgiveness – or repents and confesses before being found guilty." She also affirmed the role of justice in healing and how:

---

5. Ikiriza, *Voices of Hope*, 52.
6. Ibid., 53.

Through restorative justice, youth can regain something of what their elders lost for them in the genocide. In Rwanda, where people have killed their neighbours and cannot bring them back to life, some alternative action is needed to show they are paying a price for their actions. For example, where someone killed their neighbour, and is now repentant, they can pay school fees for the neighbour's children.[7]

After PRAY, Ikiriza went on to complete high school and a social work degree in Uganda. Then she returned to live in Rwanda. Ikiriza, along with her small team and the youth who participated in PRAY, continue to contribute to the promotion of peace in Rwanda with the generous lives they lead. Though they suffered huge losses themselves, they have devoted themselves to bringing healing, justice and peace to their beloved Rwanda. A greater emphasis on youth involvement began to emerge in the community-based work of our colleagues with specific programs for youth where they could gather and bring their views of hope and reconciliation into public life. A new program was developed where vulnerable and struggling orphans were linked with a supervized, local mentor of their choice so that they had at least one adult figure in their life as a resource and support.

The current generation of teenagers in Rwanda were born well after the genocide, and the Rwandan government is now faced with the challenge of educating them about the history and events surrounding 1994. The Commission Against Genocide now seeks ways to discuss with these youth the causes and consequences of the genocide and how it can be prevented in the future. Many of these youth have parents or relatives who were involved in, or influenced by, the work of the PRAY program. They too have a part to play in educating the next generation. The Kinyoma sector group of youth expressed it this way in 2004:

> Youth let's sit together, regardless of our ethnic groups!
> But let's build together our country, Rwanda.
> Let's design the program of unity and reconciliation even at school
> So that our children grow up in unity.
> Leaders do not leave us alone in this process of unity and
>   reconciliation
> Give time to encourage youth to build their country.

---

7. Ibid., 54.

Epilogue

"Out of disordered history a little coherence, a pattern comes,
like the steadying of a rhythm on a drum."

Wendell Berry

Discovering the Role of Umuranga

Sitting beside the pool in Kigali – the very pool in the movie 'Hotel Rwanda' that kept alive those who took refuge in Hotel Mille Colline in 1994 – I talked with my Canadian friend Gord King about Regine Uwibereyeho, the Rwandan woman he had fallen in love with while visiting a year before. Uwibereyeho had been working with the trauma team when I arrived in Rwanda. She had attended the PDW in 1997 and became the first Rwandan trained by Professor Simon to lead the workshop. With a background in psychology, she had dedicated herself to working with genocide survivors suffering from post-traumatic stress disorder – a tough task for someone who had survived the genocide herself.

Gord had returned to Rwanda to complete the ceremonies that precede a Rwandan wedding. My contribution was to serve, in part, in the role of *umuranga* (best man or best friend), acting for Gord as a go-between with the family of his bride-to-be.

As we sat sipping drinks in the late afternoon sun, I asked Gord what had attracted him to Uwibereyeho. "I saw her eyes of compassion and was drawn to the person behind that look," he said. I asked if he understood the implications of marrying a Rwandan. "My years in Latin America will help," he replied. I asked if he had organized the dowry. "Her younger male relatives have the cows in hand," he assured me. I concluded our poolside chat by pointedly asking if he was sure he wanted to follow through with the ceremony the next day. "I wouldn't miss it for all the world."

The following morning, we drove towards Butare and turned onto a side road. Gord pointed in the direction of the spot where Uwibereyeho had faced her death in 1994. Over the next three months, they slept in the bush; there Uwibereyeho lost her two brothers and many other family members. She and her sister had been discovered and marched at gunpoint with a group of fourteen other captives to a roadblock several kilometres away. There the militia began to kill the group. Amidst the chaos, the two of them had escaped, along with five others.

Traditionally, the role of *umuranga* would have included intensive research on Uwibereyeho's ancestry, as it was unacceptable to have any history of feuding between the families or any blood relative of the other party in one's family tree for the previous five generations. Obviously, these were not issues for this international marriage. Prior to any Rwandan wedding ceremony, there is the *gusaba* (asking) and the *gukwa* (dowry). Gord had the dowry covered, and I was to represent him during the asking negotiations. After a PRAY youth group sang, recited and danced, I stood to face Uwibereyeho's family and took a microphone, with Nsabiyera alongside me as my interpreter.

A representative of the bride's family began the negotiations, "We came to your office to have conversations about the plan to take away a daughter, but we did not see you there."

"I was standing on the edge of the road when I saw you coming," I replied, "but your vehicle didn't slow down. It went through a puddle and splashed my trousers, so I needed to go home and put on a clean pair for such an important meeting. My house was not far away but alas, when I returned, you were already gone!"

Another family member on the bride's side said, "We were coming to tell you that if our daughter was to leave her employment, then another member of the family would require a job. You have not shown any interest at all in that issue. We'd like to know what you could offer to us." The background laughter suggested that this exchange was going well.

"I cannot guarantee finding another job to suit your family member," I replied, "but I can assure you that if this other person has the right qualifications, we will do our best to find a place for her in our group. Please come and see me after the ceremony so we can talk further." Many smiles revealed that everyone was enjoying the spirit of this repartee. Turning to face Gord I said, "Now, I want to tell you about my clan member. Gord is a really thoughtful man who chooses carefully."

The bride's representative responded enthusiastically, "We are convinced this Gord fellow you are presenting to us is a good man, and we would like to offer him our fourth daughter. She is young, she is attractive, she is smart and she would definitely be the best choice for him. He would be pleased with her".

Even though I knew that they did not have a fourth daughter, I had to explain why she was not the right person: "No, she is too rural. He needs a city girl". The bride's family moved on to a mythical third daughter and then the second daughter, who really did exist. In each case, I had to argue about why she wouldn't fit the bill.

Finally, it was my turn to take the lead. Outlining every attribute I knew of "Her, the one who you chose to be called Uwibereyeho," I explained how she was a perfect match for Gord. "She is resilient, hard-working, a leader, trusted, wise, a healed person who helps others find their healing, a great communicator, confident speaker and besides all this she is in love with Gord. I am sure if she were here, she would confirm this."

All this time, the bride-to-be was 'hidden' inside the house, listening to the swirl of the conversation from just a few metres away. As the crowd erupted into loud applause, I looked behind me and saw Uwibereyeho being led out to sit beside Gord. The family and the community had affirmed the request for marriage!

Following the asking, we moved onto the dowry payment. Cattle are the traditional animals of choice in Rwanda, and they always will be. Three beautiful young animals were brought by young men and paraded before the family. There were more gesticulations, comments and conversations, this time about the quality of the stock, with both humorous and serious compliments revealing the obvious value that Gord placed on Uwibereyeho. All this took place over a hum of continuous banter from the crowd.

Once these negotiations concluded, the bride's side brought out an enormous clay pot filled with brewed sorghum. Individuals from each family squatted two by two and drank from the common pot with long straws of thin bamboo. After the sharing of drinks and food the rituals were concluded with a final word from the master of ceremonies: "This is a marriage of families, not of two people".

After the ceremony, many guests asked me how I had known what to say. "You know our culture. You made us all laugh," they told me. "You are a Banyarwanda, one of us!" In this joyful celebration, as we honoured the 'crowning day' when Gordon King had found his queen in Regine Uwibereyeho, I marvelled at the way I had been enfolded into this Rwandan society.

The memory of serving as an *umuranga* at the ceremony remains as one of my unforgettable Rwandan moments. I hoped that in returning to Australia, the country where I had been born, I would be able to serve as a friend and go-between, inviting others to come to know, care for and love this people and country in which I had found such belonging, welcome and home.

A Transfusion of Humanity

After living and being accepted in Rwanda, I became, as Barbara Kingsolver so eloquently wrote, impacted ". . . with Africa like a bout of a rare disease, from which I have not managed a full recovery."[1] Rwanda is my second family, where each visit begins with a "Welcome home" from my friends. They have taught me so much as we shared in our healing journeys and devoted ourselves to the work of peacebuilding. With my Rwandan colleagues, I've shared in discoveries that increased our hope and purpose in life, and deepened our desire for peace. To begin with, I have learned to reject violence as a solution. Some of Rwanda's genocide memorials remain more open to view than most war graves, and they serve as a constant reminder they were filled because of individual acts of violence. I have also learned that self-examination is the first step towards change. If we store painful hurts within ourselves, they fester and poison us. But when we examine our emotions, we can identify and confront negative forces in our lives and in our communities. Then we can be clearly guided towards positive actions. As Roméo Dallaire wrote, "We are in desperate need of a transfusion of humanity . . . proven through our actions".[2]

I also learned that we each need to take responsibility for our failures and learn from our mistakes by seeking to change our hurtful behaviour. At the same time, we need to extend forgiveness to those who have hurt us so that they can be open to change their behaviour. Rwanda developed a model of restorative justice, which freed Rwandans' energy for recovery and growth. Where punitive justice keeps injured parties at a distance from each other, restorative justice removes shame and compensates for loss. This brings the possibility of re-humanizing our relationships.

As part of the older generation, I realized that I need to make space to listen to the hope-filled vision, energy and idealism of youth. If we do not give youth freedom to create in positive ways, they will unleash their energy in negative ways – as we saw in the events in Rwanda in 1994. I also recognized the importance of honouring and remembering those who have

---

1. Barbara Kingsolver, *The Poisonwood Bible* (London: Faber & Faber, 1998), 9.
2. Dallaire, *Shake Hands with the Devil*, 522.

died. Everyone who is part of our heritage endows us with a legacy, but this gift often gets obscured by the pain of the loss and the unhealed emotions, which sidetrack our energy.

Finally, Rwanda taught me that every individual contributes to recovery. Part of our humanity is to let others be themselves. Part of our humility is to learn from the good of others. Some who were involved in the healing field described in this book have moved on. Two have left Rwanda, some have changed focus, while others remain in the work. Wherever they are, they all participated in pioneering peace efforts, which helped contribute to healing and restoration to their country.

Progress: Images of External Change

In 2012 I spent three weeks in Rwanda, retracing familiar ground and visiting my friends and colleagues after the official end of gacaca. When I landed in Kigali on the visit, I was struck by how much had changed since I arrived in 1997. Formerly dusty tracks had been paved or lined with cobblestones. High-rise buildings dotted the horizon. Vehicles and public buses filled the roads. New food and clothing markets had sprung up, along with tourism and arts initiatives. There were more police, better streetlights and traffic control, yet armed soldiers were absent from the roadsides.

As I watched planes flying into a crowded Kigali airport I heard about the new international airport to be constructed just beyond Nyamata; I was reminded of Munyeli's dream in 1997, when she imagined a future Rwanda receiving so many international visitors that a new airport would be needed. A smooth paved surface now covered the once dusty, bumpy road to Nyamata. Alongside the highway, hotels and guesthouses had sprung up, along with cement buildings for small industries. I lamented the loss of agrarian land, while acknowledging the income that tourism and manufacturing would bring to this previously marginalized area.

Rwanda continues to grow and change. Over the past twenty years, Rwanda has gone through a remarkable transformation. First and foremost this is because it developed a clear forward vision, a view of what it could become. Many long-term returnees brought back valuable education, training and business acumen to help rebuild a stronger country. Second, North America, the UK and some other countries of Europe, the Middle East and China have contributed aid, human energy and expertise. With all this energy Rwanda has become a hub of creativity, combining intellectual capacity and self-belief with human dynamism. Some speak of Rwanda as the next Switzerland, Singapore or the Dubai of Africa, as visitors pour in from around the world to enjoy its cultural and natural riches. Many surrounding African countries have taken notice of Rwanda's progress and have sent emissaries to learn from Rwanda's blossoming.[3]

Everywhere I looked I found evidences of ambition and effort. Rwandan soldiers and police are now a significant part of UN peacekeeping forces, and more women are represented in the Rwandan national parliament than any other country in the world. Rwandans have laid 3,000 kilometres of fibre optic cable to bring broadband Internet from a sub-marine cable on the East African coast. Ecologically, Rwanda is in front of many other nations, having implemented a ban on plastic bags and most polythene products, and having planted trees in order to raise the forest cover from ten percent in 2009 to thirty percent by 2020. They are now generating electrical power from methane gas tapped from Lake Kivu. The right of a woman to own land was legislated in 1999 and Rwanda has become a world-class coffee producer, partly through cooperatives of tiny farms owned by widows.

Yet, there needs to be a balance between caution and optimism. Some of the visible, physical changes in the capital city are not as present in rural areas, where poverty continues to weigh many down, and the pace of restoration is slower. I heard many comments about how hard it was for some perpetrators to make physical restitution when their own daily survival is so fragile. Moreover, almost 70 percent of the population is under the age of thirty, and there is a growing gap between the older generation, who remember the genocide, and the younger generation, who were born after 1994 – but also suffer from the after-effects on their clan and kin. Rural youth have limited opportunities and need income generating programs, while city youth need opportunities beyond tourism and unskilled manufacturing. If Rwanda is to be healed, a future hope will need to reach the youth. For as Romeo Dallaire warned in considering the lead-up to the events of 1994: "The lack of hope for the future is the root cause of rage."[4]

---

3. Wangari Maathai lists five areas of good leadership, which Africa needs. In *The Challenge for Africa*, 112–114. Several of these are evident in Rwanda.

4. Dallaire, *Shake Hands with the Devil*, 522.

Has Healing Changed People for Good?

While in this volume I've followed a tiny selection of stories, they offer shining examples of restoration across the thousands of hills that make up 'Mille Colline', the country of Rwanda. Though I do not wish to underestimate or understate the enormous need remaining in Rwanda, these stories do offer hope for the future, and the rest of the world.

After filming in 2007, I had spent time reflecting on what Rwandans had taught me. When I returned there in 2012, I wanted to find out for myself if those lessons were lasting. I spent many hours with those we had filmed in order to share the educational material we had created. I also brought them the question of some Australian students who had retorted, after listening to the presentations, "Well, I guess by now they're back at each others' throats, and fighting again . . ." As I met with Rwandans mentioned in this book, I looked for signs of deterioration, indifference or rising animosity in the storytellers.

Yet in every case I found relationships firm. The stories I had heard over the last 15 years remained true. People who had participated in healing were free from hatred and bitterness and progressing in their lives. They could talk about their freedom from spite, or they spoke about being forgiven for doing wrong, and they still appreciated and respected people who they had previously hated. People who had faced the gacaca courts and told the truth now enjoyed their eased conscience and were working to restore something of what was lost, playing their part in reforming community and rebuilding the society. Some of them were actively educating others to the importance of restored relationships. There was a general hope and optimism among these people. I could affirm that healing, repentance and forgiveness had changed these Rwandans from within – and those changes were sustained in their outward behaviour.[5]

I met with the Commissioner and Secretary General of the National Unity and Reconciliation Commission (NURC), which coordinated and documented gacaca and the impact of reconciliation efforts throughout the country. They affirmed the importance of telling the stories of hope and healing, and confirmed that more stories of the restoration of community harmony had emerged in Rwandan society, especially in rural community groups voluntarily formed to work productively together.

---

5. Other stories will be introduced on the website which accompanies this book: www.2live4give.org

I learned about the Commission against Genocide, which was created to oversee the education of all school-age children who were born after the genocide. It was a challenge to ensure that children learn about what happened, because of the possibility of raising new traumas in families who had been affected by 1994 and not received help or healing. Annie, who continued to work with the Episcopal Commission for Justice and Peace (ECJP), mentioned that post-genocide children were often told by their parents, "You don't need to know the details of what happened." So the ECJP initiated clubs at schools that treated all children as equals, rather than identifying some as the descendants of victims or perpetrators. This helped children understand the challenges of acceptance with which many of their parents still struggled.

The work of the ECJP had broadened its focus to include practical acts of restitution such as organizing workshops, and livelihood activities such as raising goats, rabbits and pigs, and teaching artisan skills such as soap making. They also offered help with conflict management among families, teaching values such as love, forgiveness, reconciliation and truth. To promote civic participation and good government, they linked self-employed people with local authorities and representatives of women, youth and the poor. They also ran good-governance workshops and explained principles of democracy to parishioners. I was impressed at these vital efforts from the much-maligned Catholic Church.

Rwanda's Hidden Challenge to Progress

During my 2012 visit, I wondered if Rwandans were aware of their ongoing need for healing. I returned to the Ntarama church memorial site with my driver and young translator, as neither had ever visited the place. They were subdued and attentive as they listened to a young guide, and I pondered the irony of the electronic world, where thousands of people from other countries had been educated about the genocide, even though some Rwandans had yet to learn the details about what had happened in their own country.

While we were discussing the memorial an older man, who was struggling under the early-afternoon effects of brewed sorghum, approached us to say, "I am one of the few survivors of the killings in this church. I was hidden under a mass of bodies and escaped death. But don't feel sorry for me. The people you should be sorry for are those who committed the atrocities – they must have such a terrible weight on their conscience. Many of them languish in prison. What a hopeless life they live."

Memorial site at Ntarama church   © Dave Fullerton

This is an example of the other side of the picture, for the majority of Rwandans, as in most countries post-war, have had limited opportunity to experience healing. Many have not had the time to look into their past and understand its ongoing impact in themselves. Any person who presses on with life without healing the past and leaving behind the poison, is not able to live into the full hope and experience of a good future. Thus a country may be functioning and stable, but many of its people may not be.

Though the focus on reconciliation and restoration is alive and well in Rwanda, there remains the risk of moving ahead without transforming hearts.

Seeds of Hope and Generosity

In writing this book, it is my hope that readers will go beyond merely admiring the beauty that is growing out of the lives of the Rwandan people whose stories are collected here. For these Rwandans have offered their experiences as gifts to be grasped with both hands, inviting transformation rather than passive armchair reading 'voyeurism'. In attending to these lives, which have sprouted out of the rubble of the horrors and violence of genocide, we must each consider how healing, forgiveness and transformation might be possible as we carry the weight, wounds and poison of our daily 'wars': the conflicts, annoyances, slights or misunderstandings.

When we examine the ways in which Rwandans have embarked on the painful journey of seeking healing in their own lives and in their battered country, we can learn how to nurture our healing, find and extend forgiveness, and minimize conflict in our own part of the world. The principles of recovery in Rwanda translate into principles of prevention and cure for the rest of us.

After one woman had completed a healing workshop, her husband contacted the facilitator and said, "Thank you for the work you did with my wife. The impact is obvious, she is noticeably different. Now I need something to heal myself. Please give me the same medicine." Rwandans use natural medicines, potions and herbs to promote healing. As Buhanda said, "But, when you want to heal, you take medicine, and most medicines are not sweet." In human recovery, it often tastes bitter to focus on our own stories, rather than on those of our scapegoats or victims. But when we examine and work with the hurt, pain and poison that is within us, we embark on our own healing journeys. Here, we may see the healing Rwandans as our *umuranga* – a best friend who beckons us to sip together from the pot that brings two sides together. If we do this we partner with those who have already stepped across the divide, which separates denial and revenge from forgiveness and reconciliation.

"Generosity begins with someone taking a risk, making a gesture," writes Dave Toycen.[6] Rwanda's road to generosity is not a self-help recipe; rather, it invites us to take the risk and experience change in ourselves, and then reach out to others with an open and spacious heart. Such charity and kindness has helped transform pockets of Rwanda. If we are willing, these seeds of hope, which are sprouting out of the bloodied Rwandan soil, can scatter across barriers, borders, and continents and bring fresh shoots of life and hope to our world.

---

6. Dave Toycen, *The Power of Generosity* (Nashville: Harper Collins, 2004), 50.

A Rwandan Responds

It has been a great pleasure reading *From Genocide to Generosity*. John Steward is a faithful and wonderful storyteller. Recounting our story is what has kept many of us Rwandans in our sanity, despite the unimaginable cruelties we witnessed through the 100 days of the genocide against the Tutsis and the war that brought it to an end. Trusted contexts helped us to dispel the culture of silence we inherited from our ancestors, and telling our stories helped us heal from our traumas.

I have worked in different positions that have put me in the forefront of the reconciliation process in Rwanda. I, myself, am a survivor of the genocide who learned to heal and forgive. I'm a preacher of the healing message of the cross of Jesus Christ and have been a Commissioner on the National Unity and Reconciliation Commission for twelve years. I was Vice-Chair of the Commission for three terms. I know first-hand what this book is trying to convey and most of the people spoken about are friends with whom I've laboured in the healing of our nation.

Our hearts are fragile and we all get wounded. What causes the bleeding may differ but the resulting pain is the same and the healing process goes through the same steps. Finding a safe place to tell my story, processing the depth of my wound and shaping a future that is not fettered by the strings that bind me to the hurtful event is the healing secret for a hurting world. But nothing does it better than standing before the cross of Jesus Christ!

Thank you John for taking this message to the world. In Rwanda, we talk but we are not very good at writing. By writing this book, you are serving us by celebrating these 'heroes' who will never write their own stories and you are serving the whole world by showing them that there is hope even after the furnace of genocide. I trust this book will be of use to many people.

Antoine Rutayisire
Senior Pastor, Remera Anglican Parish
& Principal, Kigali Anglican Theological College
October 6, 2014

Acknowledgements

I acknowledge retired Lieutenant-General Roméo Dallaire for your fortitude, empathy, personal suffering and great example in not deserting Rwanda in its time of need. On the back cover of your book you wrote, "This is . . . the account of a few humans who were entrusted with the role of helping others taste the fruits of peace." I hope you find here a satisfying sequel.

To Father Michael Lapsley for your example of courage, honesty and compassion and for the Foreword.

To Sandi my partner and courageous friend in all this work. You know what we experienced together; we would not have chosen this adventure for ourselves, but were drawn there by a higher call.

To my parents Harrold (†) & Gwenda (†) who introduced me to the Christ-life of faith, purpose and adventure.

To family and friends who did not challenge our decision to move to Rwanda in 1997 and who supported us over the crests and through the valleys.

To Dave and Sally who helped translate Rwandans' message to youth in ways that they could hear, creating the award-winning educational website www.rwandanstories.org. They have given me regular and steady support, and created my new website to accompany this volume: www.2live4give.org.

To the people of Truth and Liberation Concern, St John's Cranbourne, Christchurch Tooradin and the Melbourne Anglican Foundation for your prayerful and practical support.

To World Vision who made this work possible, and especially Norbert, Nyamugasira (†), Mukandekezi, Dave T, Fisseha, Lynn, Frank, Gabby, Debbie, Evelyne, Rulinda (†), Edwin & Martha, Lincoln, Marionne, Kofi, Muheri, Kalisa, Mutabazi, Gasatura, Musoni, Gatera, Mbabazi and Mukanwezi.

To Bosco (†), Faustin and Adrian and all the friendly staff at IRIS guesthouse for your loyal service.

To Phil & Nikki for good conversations and kicking goals in Rwanda.

To Mike & Rosalie for keeping the news flowing to our support base.

To Rob and Carol, Josh, Ken and Di, Rowan, Kristin, Simone, Bryan and Janet, Geoff & Robin, David and Sylvia, Ruth and Lis for your solidarity and feedback. To all who perused and endorsed the manuscript.

To David, Dianne, Ted (†), Sharon and Sue for your attention to listening and wise input.

To Adele, Esther, Andy, Alexander and the team at Living Well Centre for Christian Spirituality for your sustained interest in my life and work.

To Methode & Mary, Karl & Deb, Lincoln and Tito for your sanity and hospitality.

To the 'Holy Scribblers' and 'Word Weavers' writers' groups for inspiration, guidance and networks.

To Karen Hollenbeck Wuest for patiently and skilfully turning a stodgy manuscript into a nourishing volume.

To Annthea Hick (of AHCreative) for her brilliant and perceptive graphic design for the cover.

To David Fullerton, Colin Smith, Jon Warren/World Vision & Lyndon Mechielsen for photographs.

To Pieter Kwant for suggesting the title and, with Luke Lewis and Vivian Doub, bringing this volume into the world of marketing.

To my Rwandan family, I honour you for working to bring hope through healing, first in your own lives and then for others. I hold each one of you in high regard. You are amazing.

Amakuru, Imana Ishimwe cani.

Glossary

ECJP - Episcopal Commission for Justice and Peace in the Catholic Church.

Gacaca – the community based (grassroots) traditional method conflict resolution, literally meaning 'on the grass', which was re-modelled by the Government of Rwanda to become a quasi-legal process for bringing participants of the genocide to trial, with a focus on restorative justice.

HOM – Healing of Memories, 3-day workshop for interfaith audiences developed in South Africa by Father Michael Lapsley.

HWEC – Healing the Wounds of Ethnic Conflict, a 3-day workshop developed in Rwanda by Dr Rhiannon Lloyd for church leaders and laity.

Interahamwe – a Kinyarwanda word for 'those who stand/fight together'; the Hutu youth militias trained with the help of French aid to attack Tutsi to further the goal of genocide.

Inyangamugayo – a Kinyarwanda word for 'wise or respected elder'; those elected as judges for the gacaca process, based on their standing in the community, dedication to the well-being of their neighbours and love of truth and justice.

Mille Colline – the French name of a hotel; also a favoured description of Rwanda: "Land of a thousand hills".

Muzungu – white person, wealthy one, foreigner.

NGO – Non-Governmental Organization.

NURC – National Unity and Reconciliation Commission, the government body overseeing and documenting reconciliation in Rwanda.

PDW – Personal Development Workshop, an 11-day healing program in four steps, developed in Rwanda by Professor Simon Gasibirege for a general audience.

PRAY – Promotion of Reconciliation Among Youth, program led by Annet Ikiriza where youth created and performed messages of change and peace using arts expression.

Refugee, long-term – about 1 million Rwandans who fled the country and lived in exile as a result of the cycles of killing from 1952 onwards; also known as "the Tutsi diaspora", although not exclusively Tutsi.

Refugee, short-term – Up to 2.5 million Rwandans, mostly Hutu, who fled to surrounding African countries in 1994 in fear of reprisal attacks from the RPF or revenge from survivors. The largest number camped in Zaire [now Congo] in terrible conditions and most returned to Rwanda in late 1996 after RPF intervention.

RPF – Rwanda Patriotic Front, the armed force gathered in exile from long-term Rwandan refugees (mostly Tutsi, some Hutu) who invaded Rwanda from the north in 1990 and signed a power sharing peace accord in Arusha with the Rwandan government in 1993. Led by General Paul Kagame the RPF army liberated Rwanda from Hutu control and formed the basis of the new government in 1994.

Rwandanstories.org – the award-winning website of videos and curriculum, which offers material for study on the genocide to English speaking, secondary schoolteachers.

Survivor – any person in Rwanda who was attacked or in danger of losing their lives during the genocide or any person who lost loved ones during, before or after the 100 days of 1994.

TRC – the Truth and Reconciliation Commission in South Africa, which oversaw the post-apartheid program.

UKA – *Ukuri Kuganze*, meaning 'Let truth prevail'; an Association of over 2000 Rwandans promoting healing, reconciliation and recovery at the grassroots in Nyamata and elsewhere in the country.

UN – United Nations.

Vanishing Point – a curriculum for English speaking high school students based on the genocide, its causes and recovery; available through the rwandanstories.org website.

Index of Rwandans

Ahimana – NGO manager of the Ruhengeri region; husband of Makoriko, 69-70, 72, 78

Annie Kaligirwa – Coordinator of the healing and reconciliation program of the Episcopal Catholic Commission for Justice and Peace, 130, 164

Bembereza – Jailed in Gisenyi for a minor offence, but confessed publicly to killing Delphina's father and offered her restitution in kind, 113-115, 143

Buhanda – Survivor from Nyamata. Secretary of *Ukuri Kuganze* Association, 121, 123-124, 166

Deborah, Mama – mother from Ruhengeri who, because of a dream, forgave the soldier who shot her son and adopted him as a replacement son, 85-93, 115

Delphina – Student from Gisenyi. She forgave Bembereza, who killed her father, 114-115, 143

Drusilla – Field staff from the south near Butare who experienced healing in the PDW, 52

Ikiriza – Child welfare officer who traced unaccompanied children; she joined the peacebuilding team to coordinate PRAY project, 8, 137-143, 146-147, 151, 153-155, 171

Iramuremye Saulve – Holy man, martyred in west Rwanda; father of Munyeli, 48-49

Jean-Baptiste Ntakirutimana – Survivor who joined the peacebuilding team and reconciled with the man who killed his mother, 8, 78, 94-97, 100-103

Josephine – Field staff in Byumba, who reconciled with her enemies after attending the PDW, 23-28

Karigirwa – Member of the trauma team and facilitator of the PDW, 8, 33, 36-47, 51

Karinda – Young man from Lake Muhazi region, who confessed to killing Saverina's son; they reconciled and tell their story to others, 127, 129-131

Makoriko – Widow who married Ahimana of Ruhengeri in 1997. After healing she develops a friendship with Mama Deborah, 69-72, 92-93

Mukarurinda – Mother from Nyamata who reconciled with Ndayisaba who cut off her hand, 124-127, 136

Munyeli – Joined the peacebuilding team to coordinate the PDW. Left in 2000 to prepare Rwanda for gacaca; rejoined the peacebuilding team in 2005 to continue facilitating healing programs, 8, 33, 49-52, 109-110, 112, 120, 131-133, 135, 161

Musabyimana – From Nyamata; one of the first prisoners to tell the truth; reconciled with Buhanda, whom he attacked and whose sister he killed, 121-124

Ndayisaba – From Nyamata; a man who killed many. He cut off Mukarurinda's hand; later he reconciled with her, 124, 126-127

Ndogoni – Psychologist from Kenya who headed the trauma department, 13, 28, 146

Nsabiyera – Psychologist who moved from the trauma department to join the peacebuilding team, 8, 20, 25, 78-83, 85, 87, 95, 158

Nyamutera – The first Hutu facilitator of the HWEC in Rwanda, 8, 53, 58-71, 76, 83, 101, 103

Rutimburana – NGO manager of the Byumba region, 135, 137

Sabamungu – Interpreter and first Rwandan facilitator of the HWEC, 64, 68, 70, 73, 75

Saverina – Mother from Lake Muhazi region, who forgave Karinda after he admitted killing one of her sons; they spoke about their reconciliation in public and in prisons, 127-131

Simon Gasibirege –Psychologist and professor from Butare who developed the PDW. Now manager of the 'Life Wounds Recovery Centre', 8, 15, 171

Uwibereyeho – Survivor who joined the trauma team. The first NGO facilitator of the PDW, 157-159

Index of Places of Rwanda

Appendix

The Twelve-Step Process of Forgiveness

In Rwanda people generally resist the idea of forgiveness. Some churches contributed to the fear of forgiveness by persistent calls for victims to 'forgive and forget'; this only increased the burden of pain among survivors. I noticed that attitude in our Personal Development Workshop (PDW). Participants expected something demanding or condemnatory; but I observed a freeing influence within the group as they saw new wisdom placed in front of them. The following handout on the topic of forgiveness, which commenced the fourth stage workshop of the PDW, was well received because of its good sense, deep compassion and lack of pressure:

Forgiveness is not a unique [single/simple] act, but more a kind of inner pilgrimage, to:
1. Not take revenge and to cease offensive actions. The walk towards forgiveness begins with two decisions – to decide not to seek revenge, and to stop the offensive situation. There is no point in wanting to forgive if the offensive situation is going on.
2. Recognize our inner wounds. If we deny our pain and hide the wound, we also bar the possibility of healing. This person has hurt me/is hurting me, they have offended me, and I suffer because of this. Denying, minimizing or avoiding are defence mechanisms that prevent us from reaching real forgiveness. They hold the energy inside us.
3. Share our inner wound with someone. Rather than bear the wound all by ourselves, tell the story to someone who will listen and not judge, or moralize or give advice. This allows us to see the situation in a larger perspective. Every telling both shares our pain and allows the story to lose a little of its power over us.

4. Identify the loss and grieve it. List all the losses caused by the offence and grieve for what you have lost. Weep, wail, mourn, and reminisce.

5. Accept the anger and the desire for revenge. It is natural, but it does not have to push us to destructive actions. Anger is there to express the need for justice; we need to fully imagine vengeance in images. Slowly the images will go.

6. Forgive myself. We feel guilt, shame and blame, a desire for revenge – these feelings affect our inner harmony and they need forgiveness, as do our mistakes. To forgive myself is the first condition allowing me to forgive others.

7. Understand our offender. Put aside blame and place oneself in the other's position – imagine their suffering, realizing what they did is irreversible. Recognize their value as a human being; accept their mystery.

8. Find some meaning for the offence in our life. With time we might see some positive value or meaning to what happened. But this cannot be felt straight after the event.

9. Know that we are worthy of forgiveness and already forgiven. Each of us has been forgiven many times; forgiveness gives us dignity and a sense of value. For those who accept the idea of a God who forgives, there is the possibility to feel accepted unconditionally.

10. Stop pursuing forgiveness. Forgiveness is not a moral obligation. We cannot demand it from others. Not all people are ready to forgive – they do not respond to pressure. The process takes time and everyone has their own process. Pressure adds guilt and builds the wall of resistance and resentment.

11. Open myself to the grace to forgive. It is not natural, it is beyond comprehension – we don't understand in advance how we will forgive. We often need to call on divine help.

12. Decide to end the relationship/friendship or renew it. If forgiveness leads to reconciliation, it is impossible to meet each other in the way it was before the offence. The relationship will begin on a new basis. Forgiveness may be given and the relationship ends, for different reasons. It is still beneficial for the offended and the offender.

Poletti and Dobbs developed this material from a French text by John Monbourquette, which was subsequently published in English (see Bibliography). For further information go to www.2live4give.org

Bibliography

Augsburger, David W. *Helping People Forgive*. Louisville: Westminster John Knox Press, 1996.

Bartlett, John. *Bartlett's Familiar Quotations*. New York: Little, Brown and Company, 1968.

Church, J. E. *Forgive Them: The Story of an African Martyr*. London: Hodder & Stoughton, 1966.

Clark, Philip. *The Gacaca Courts, Post-Genocide Justice and Reconciliation in Rwanda*. Cambridge: Cambridge University Press, 2010.

Clark, Philip, and Zachary D. Kaufman, eds. *After Genocide: Transitional Justice, Post-conflict Reconstruction and Reconciliation in Rwanda and Beyond*. London: Hurst Publishers, 2008.

Dallaire, Romeo. *Shake Hands with the Devil: The Failure of Humanity in Rwanda*. New York: Carroll and Graf Publishers, 2003.

Des Forges, Alison. *Leave none to tell the story*. New York: Human Rights Watch, 1999.

Fullerton, Dave. *Rwandanstories.org*, Melbourne, 2010.

Gashumba, Frida. *Frida: Chosen to Die, Destined to Live*. Lancaster: Sovereign World, 2007.

Ikiriza, Annet. *Voices of Hope*. World Vision Rwanda, 2003.

Kapuściński, Ryszard. *The Shadow of the Sun*. London: Penguin Books, 2001.

Keane, Fergal. *Season of Blood: A Rwandan Journey*. London: Viking, 1995.

Kingsolver, Barbara. *The Poisonwood Bible*. London: Faber & Faber, 1998.

Koff, Clea. *The Bone Woman*. London: Hodder & Stoughton, 2004.

Lapsley, Michael. "Bicycle Theology." *Sunday Independent*. Column. 2000 (June 11).

———. *Redeeming the Past*. Maryknoll: Orbis, 2012.

Maathai, Wangari. *The Challenge for Africa*. London: Arrow Books, 2009.

Mbanda, Laurent. *Committed to Conflict*. London: SPCK, 1997.

Monbourquette, John. *How to Forgive: A Step-by-Step Guide*. London: Darton Longman & Todd, 2000.

Smedes, Lewis B. *The Art of Forgiving: When You Need to Forgive and Don't Know How*. Melbourne: Summit Publishing, 1996.

Toycen, Dave. *The Power of Generosity*. Nashville: Harper Collins, 2004.

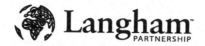**Langham** PARTNERSHIP

Langham Partnership is working to strengthen the church in the majority world. We provide doctoral scholarships for future principals and teachers at majority world seminaries and for those who will take up strategic positions of leadership in the church. We send carefully chosen evangelical books, as gifts or at low cost, to church pastors and to teachers at Bible colleges, and we foster the writing and publishing of Christian literature in many regional languages. We also run training workshops and produce materials to raise the standard of biblical preaching and teaching, and work to develop preaching networks locally. For further information see www.langham.org or email global@langham.org

---

2live4give.org

A fresh website moderated by John Steward for:

- your feedback about this book and how it impacted you
- your questions and experience about forgiveness
- a study guide to use with the book, and questions for discussion in reading groups
- enquiry, dialogue, quotes, thoughts and reflections on bringing healing and hope into our world
- new material for interfaith groups & workshop leaders

Watch for regular updates and new stories from Rwanda and elsewhere in the world.
Like "From Genocide to Generosity" on Facebook or comment on Twitter #FmGen2Gen

Healing and forgiveness brings us back to life

CPSIA information can be obtained
at www.ICGtesting.com
Printed in the USA
LVOW13s1918120717

541118LV00019B/1339/P